"DOES POPCORN COME FROM AN EGG?"

STORIES ABOUT THREE CHILDREN AND THEIR GR'AUNTIE

BY

RITA BRESNAHAN

Book and Cover Design: Vladimir Verano, Third Place Press

Cover photography : © Rita Bresnahan

Author photo © Rita Bresnahan

Author contact: *namaste7@comcast.net*

ISBN: 978-0-9899881-1-7

Printed at Third Place Press, Lake Forest Park, WA on the Espresso Book Machine v.2.2. www.thirdplacepress.com

To Emma, Ethan, and Chloe
and
to children everywhere…

May we honor your presence
and your precious spirit…

May we listen closely to your wisdom
and deep questions,
as you remind us
how to be in this world…

CONTENTS

GRATITUDES   *i*

PREFACE   *iii*

THE THREE CHILDREN   *1*

Enter Emma
   Welcome to Toddlerville
Enter Ethan
   Second Childhood?
Enter Chloe
   All Is Well
You Are My Sunshine

THE WORLD THROUGH A CHILD'S EYES   *21*

Lullaby
"Does Popcorn Come From an Egg?"
A Fire! A Fire!
"How Much Is That Dog-gie in the Window?"
A Firetruck! A Firetruck!
The Lens
Happy Hour
"Who's in Charge of You?"
Some Questions Are Best Unanswered
I'm All Ears
It's the Police!
Fashionista? Not!
Computer Magic

When Someone Is Hurting 47

Band-Aid

Lavender Brushing

Reunion

Purple Toe LTC

Miracle Worker

Whatever Works

Pause

Showing Kindness 63

A Catalog of Kindnesses

"Take This Home With You"

Taking Turns: Skippy Comes To Visit

The Microphone Tree

"Are You Okay?"

Counting Kindnesses

Behind My Pillow

The World of Feelings 79

"I'm Sorry"

"Are You Happy?"

"Where Is My Fa-mi-ly?"

Puzzled

"God in My Heart"

Upset

Feelings Can Change in a Flash

"I'm Scared"

Love Is in the Air

Out And About   101

Dandelion Pillow
"Weeds Are Flowers Too…"
Falling in Love With Her Shadow
Moonstruck
Happy Blooms
Sam the Moth

Together, We Learn   117

Emma Stands Her Ground
Tomorrow, Tomorrow…
Two Neighbors
Mirror Mirror on the Wall
It's Okay to Be Okay
Highest, Biggest, Fastest, Kindest
"If You Ever Want to See Me Again…"
"I Am Reading!"
Try, Try Again
Screen Time, Our Time

Reflections   139

"Am I Old?"
Next?
A "Good" Time
Epiphany
Legacy: "I can write a story!"
Upward

A Blessing   157
Resources   159
About the Author   163

GRATITUDES

To my Co-authors:
Emma, Ethan, and Chloe,
>who keep me singing and dancing
>and honest
>giggling and young at heart

~ To their mommy and daddy
>who always welcome me
>into their home

~ To my sister Mary
>for sharing her grandchildren with me
>for her fine organizing and editing

~ To generous readers/friends
>Claire, Jeanette, Barb, Alison, Jeanne,
>Roselle, Mary Ann, Mary, Shelly, Peggy

~ To Deb and Ed
>for keeping my body and soul together
>during intense writing times

PREFACE

At the ripe old age of 75, I learned a new skill. Previously, I had made only brief skirmishes into that foreign land: the world of sewing.

Back in 7th grade when I was forced to take Home Ec's 4-week sewing unit, since I wanted to pass, I managed to make an apron. A half-apron really. It was red with tiny white snowflakes. Even my mother had a difficult time wearing it.

In 1975 when I was in the hospital for lung surgery, to help me pass the time, my sister gave me one of those hooking-rug kits, replete with fancy yarns, a stamped pattern (on primitive burlap), a color key, and a rug hook. The scene was a windmill, in oranges and browns. I went at it with such a vengeance that all the nurses dubbed me "the Mad Hooker." The masterpiece never quite made it into the frame that came with the kit.

A few years later, recuperating from another surgery, I was given an embroidery packet. Complete with lovely threads and just the right size needles, the kit held a stamped pattern of a colorless garden waiting to be made beautiful. It stared up at me, hopeful, quivering. I tried my best, but once again, had to abort the project early in the process, because I

    a. Sewed several stitches to the hospital gown beneath the hoop, and

    b. Gouged the needle into my cheek on a particularly vigorous upswing stitch.

That pretty much sums up my sewing history. Not a thing I can think of could coax me back into that arena... but... well, a new baby coming. In the family. Only minutes from me. To welcome the wee one, my long-time neighbor and friend Shelly encouraged me to make a receiving blanket, and even volunteered to serve as coach. Thus it was that in November I set out to learn to use a sewing machine.

First Shelly had me practice stitching on paper. Poor ole Singer. How it galloped and lurched in great starts and stops, often running away from me. For two sessions, my coach, a seasoned seamstress herself, assessed the situation, then noted sensitively, "Maybe we'd better start out just making burp rags." I'd never heard of such. Nor was I offended.

Off we went to the nearby fabric store. I had not been inside such a dizzying visual world before, and I held tightly on to Shelly's belt as she led me through the maze to: baby fabrics. I was amazed at the choices: soft mellow colors, fleecy pastels. Rubbing one after another between my fingers, a brilliant idea came to me: personalize those burp cloths! Choose materials like one with footballs for the new daddy, three with "I Love Grandma", one with fancy cars for Grandpa, one with sassy cats for Gr'auntie (me) etc. So that's what I did.

It took me ten (10) burp cloths to get the hang of it. Nevertheless, I faithfully dug multi-colored zig-zags all around those 12 by 8's. All around. And around. And around. Finally I graduated to the receiving blanket! It was all a labor of love. Shelly hovered close by to correct snafus, at times resorting to the quick ripper. She'd fill the bobbin when it ran out, or feed the needle when the thread popped; she'd adjust the stitch size or zig-zag knob. Some fifteen hours she kept watch, getting me around thick corners, all the humps. "That's what friends are for," she reminded me, "to help one another over the rough spots."

In early December of 2008 my fortune cookie message read: "A short stranger will soon appear in your life bringing many blessings." Sure enough, little Emma Grace arrived a week later, on December 8! My grandniece!

As I cradle sweet Emma, I just gaze and gaze at this little being, so close to The Light. And I've wept more than a bit. Poet John O'Donohue imagines a child entering this world praying:

> *...May my eyes never lose sight*
> *of why I have come here...*
> *In everything I do, think,*
> *feel, and say,*
> *May I allow the light*
> *of the world I am leaving*
> *to shine through and carry me home.*

These words speak to me. Their meaning begins to expand and seep into my own life, for they reveal my mission too. No matter where on the life spectrum we find ourselves—at the beginning, in the middle, or toward the end—I believe we are called to remember and live from that exquisite place in ourselves: the presence and spirit that defines who we really are: the golden thread that weaves itself from the beginning of our days through to the end. Each of is the same blessed essence today as when we entered this world...the same blessed essence as when we depart...

This truth is both humbling and comforting. I too find myself intoning the prayer:

> *"May my eyes never lose sight of why I have come to earth:*
> *To love. To serve.*
> *To allow the Light within*
> *to keep shining through..."*

2015: The soft fleecy blanket, and the prayers too,
wrapped Emma round about for many months.
They also brought comfort to her little brother
and sister who followed: Ethan, twenty months later,
and Chloe, a year after that.
The ten burp cloths were also happy to be of service
throughout all those years!

THREE CHILDREN

Enter Emma

DECEMBER 8, 2008 Emma burst into our world! Emma! Emma Grace—the family's first little Northwest baby girl! Such a beautiful baby, born on such a special day: a Mother Mary feast day.

My sister Mary being her Grandma made me Emma's Gr'auntie. For the first time ever, there'd be a baby in the family close to where I lived. Maybe I can be a part of her life!

I was thrilled at the thought.

Emma was soooo tiny. Everybody wanted to hold her, so we had to take turns. We would all sing to her, and cuddle her, and Mommy pumped a lot of milk for her. From her first days, she was interactive, so responsive to the person holding her. She really looked at you. And her eyes just sparkled! The way she moved her hands around was so graceful for such a tiny one. Even her pediatrician commented on her expressive baby hands.

Soon after her birth, it was apparent that this little baby had problems keeping her food down. It would take almost an hour for her to take even one ounce. She fussed and cried during her feedings and it was difficult to watch. She eventually was hospitalized. Her devoted parents stayed with her in the room, and meticulously followed every directive they were given by the medical team. Emma was a survivor, and eventually began gaining weight. How relieved we were!

Now this is remarkable: Emma began liking books when she was only six weeks old! She would look and look, and seem as if she understood. She loved to have stories read to her. And how she loved to twirl around, even as a baby; she twirled and twirled, especially around in the kitchen in her mommy's arms. How much she likes to dance today!

Emma came to us only three weeks before Christmas, and she was our best Christmas present ever! She blesses our whole family.

Welcome to Toddlerville

I find myself knee-deep in Toddlerville these days.
With ten toddlers in music class
    (imagine—ten!)
drumming dancing scarfing peekabooing rocking.

Fifteen toddlers in swimming class
    kickingbubblingjumping spattering sputtering
        making water their friend.

At home—throwing, no-ing
    running chasing "I'm gonna get yous" hiding hiding
        on the move without cease.
            Chaos, utter chaos.

                    A toddler miracle occurred yesterday
                        during my Emma watch.

Suddenly, in the midst of her whirlwind,
    Emma pulled the fuzzy red pillow onto the floor,
        lay her head down on it, and stretched out,
            eyes wide open.
                She wasn't sleepy.

She lay that way for ten minutes or so, ten minutes!
    not making a sound,
looking at me, and past me,
    into some far-away place.

And I—for those same ten minutes,
    gazed back softly at her, and past her…
        into some far-away place.

We just let one another be, be, be…
    knowing what we needed at that moment,
        and honoring that.

That is where we meet the most,
        she and I,
    in that place filled with breath and silence.

The urge might be to tickle her
    or engage her in some way…draw her out…
        but no, I must not.
            She is the guide.

Her mommy comes back after a while.
        My watch is over.

As I am leaving, she wonders aloud,

"Rita, you're one of Emma's favorites.

Do you know what makes your relationship so special?"

Oh, I cannot count the ways.

How describe the secret hollow

where we two meet?

the place of silence and breath and calm,

oft forgotten in Toddlerville,

quite rare these days as well, in a society

needing to be constantly on the move

or entertained.

Emma and I, we share a quiet slowing-down tender place

where we listen without words

and see beyond what is visible,

a luminous state

where we toddle along together—

in the dawn of her life…

and the evening of mine…

Enter Ethan

❧

A remarkable day to be born! An article in the Seattle Times that day headlines: CLEAR SKIES LIGHT UP WITH METEORS. "Clear, moonless night skies make for spectacular stargazing this week as the annual Perseid meteor showers light up the night. The best viewing will be outside the cities, and after midnight. The peak of the showers, when as many as 60 shooting stars an hour might be seen, is predicted for Thursday night…"

The last weeks of pregnancy have been scary, and Michelle has been on bed rest—not easy with a toddler around, but she did want her baby to be full-term. We anxiously waited…Would this baby be okay?

And he made it! What a joy it was to look at his sweet round face. He was healthy. He was eating well. What a huge relief! After only two days, Ethan was able to come home. Emma, at twenty months, did her best to welcome him, pat-patting him, though at times a little too vigorously. She was sure he would be leaving any day. But he stayed. And giggled. Made Emma giggle too. Giggling giggling became his trademark.

"Ethan" was the name of a wise man in the Old Testament. It means "Solid, enduring, firm, strong." Okay, that sounds just right for this little boy to grow into...

An idea: Let's watch the shooting stars every year on his birthday! Wouldn't that be a grand way to celebrate!

The day he was born was indeed glorious: the sky was clear…with an astonishing swirl of stars shimmering.

And shooting stars for Baby Ethan—tracing his name across the skies.

A star is born!

Second Childhood?

How can time be so mistaken?
It says I'm 80!
        80 years old.

How then, why then,
    do I still talk to and giggle with Elmo?
            Station stuffed animals to keep watch during lunch
                cheering and clapping when bites of protein go down

Why, if I'm 80, do I play "Go Fish" and "Slapjack" with such gusto
    (but not "Old Maid", even though someone had the gall to
include such a deck in the set I bought…)

Or like yesterday,
        when I heard a rare pinging at the window,
why do I throw open the front door
        and shout excitedly, "Come 'ere! Come 'ere!"
    … so four tiny feet and two big ones could stand at the
threshold letting hail
        pelt bare toes
    …so we could pick up tiny ice pellets,
            hold them and gaze at them
                put them up to our cheeks
                    as they melt away…
and we are shouting, "Hail! Hail! It's hailing!"
        … in awe… as if for the first time…

We got a little cold then, and with great reluctance, we close the door.
"Hail is rain that comes down like tiny pieces of ice!" Ethan exclaims.

Why, if I really am 80
    do I get excited at sirens in the distance
        at crows waiting at the curb for cars to pass
            and blowing dandelion puffs in the alley

Why, why at this advanced age—
        am I now prompted to start moving and dancing at the
first sound of music?
And go around humming tunes like "Twinkle Twinkle little star…"
and ABCDEFG…"

Why, every day,
    do I find cooky crumbs in my pocket
        and cheddar goldfish too.

Why **ever** do I find myself down on the floor so often these days—
        when I haven't fallen there…(and the getting up is not so
easy…)
Why am I…
    why do I…
        why…why…why…

Could it be…I am in my second childhood?

I don't know. I don't know what to call this wondrous stage.

Perhaps…
      simply…name it
            Love.

Yes, that's what I'll call it.
            Love.

      No other word will do.

Enter Chloe

Chloe burst into the world mid-morning on OCTOBER 10, 2011

Weighing 5 pounds, 4 ounces.

The baby is taken directly into the neo-natal ICU, with trouble breathing, and rapid heart-beat. She has to stay in the hospital.

Meanwhile, back at her house, Emma plays "hold baby sister" many times. Wraps a blanket up the way Chloe will be, and rocks and rocks. Sometimes we put Elmo in a blanket for extra practice. Emma rocks some more and softly sings "Twinkle Twinkle Little Star." She is gentle, so affectionate, putting the "baby" up to her cheek and kissing her.

Ethan, meanwhile, is pretty nonchalant about the blessed event. At 14 months, a newcomer doesn't seem to make much difference to him.

After three weeks in the hospital, Chloe's relieved parents are able to bring their little one home. There is still concern about how distended her stomach is, and the parents are told to watch her very carefully. X-ray shows one huge bubble remains in her stomach.

When they come in the front door, Emma shouts, "Baby sister, baby sister, I love you. I like you. I love you!" "You are sooooo tiny!"

She gets to hold Chloe, wants Chloe to sleep with her, keeps tiptoeing in to peek at her in the crib. She sings to her softly. The sister bond grows strong.

Ethan often stands and looks and looks at Chloe, especially when she's in the crib.

Sometimes he reaches in between the slats and gently touches her little hand.

For a kiss, he "head bumps" her, also very gently, or pat-pats her on the head.

Out in the wide wide world, the autumn leaves are bursting into flaming colors everywhere to celebrate this newborn child.

All Is Well

The two of us start out...
   ever
     so
       slowly
         down the front walk...

Without even looking,
   she holds up to me one toddler hand...
      yes, without looking up...
trusting...
  knowing... I am there...
  and will grasp her hand...
    and hold on tight.

        All is well in her world.
          No harm shall come...

We toddle along the walk
   at her pace
bending down to admire
  and run our hands through
    tiny tufts of grass here
      and mini daisies there...
  I would have passed them right by.
We giggle at each bow-wow that lopes along,
  and point excitedly at squawking crows.

(Oh look and see, really look and see!)

...I imagine
as similar
my walk with the Divine,
the Mystery,
That Which Holds Us All...

I need not look up or around to see,
or wonder if that Presence dwells nearby..
I reach out...
I trust...
I am held...

It is I who set the pace of my walk,
though not its length...
and I marvel without cease
the bountiful world,
the simple gifts laid gently at my feet.

You Are My Sunshine

Hello sun in my cereal
   cereal in my hair
      cream cheese on my knees,
hello sun on the teddy grahams
      you plop on the floor…
hello sun when you're hiding
   with your blankie sticking out
beaming full sun when you're found.

Sun as you put your whole face in the wee bag
      where cheerios are hidden.
Grinning at your find,
  with deft fingers you pluck them out,
   one by one
offering me an "o" as if it were a great treasure—
   and it is.

Best professors I ever had
  even in grad school.

You give me A's.
A—for fresh eyes to see the little treasures
A—reminding me what really matters
A—for finding stamina when I think I've run out.
    Patience too
A—calling forth a kind of love from depths unknown
A—for playing, being silly, laugh laughing

You make the morning happy
　　and the tender nights too.
　　　　"Ni' ni'" Cuddlebug, cuddle.

You are generous beyond words,
offering not only cheerio or toy,
　　but your whole being
　　　　gives and gives.
　　　　　　There's no holding back.

You ease us all with your warm touch
　　your soft pat-pats, your big hugs and holy kiss
　　　　even your tiny pinches. Ouch!

You hold us in your tiny hands of light.
　　　　You bless our worlds.

THE WORLD THROUGH
A CHILD'S EYES

Lullaby

I am sitting in the big chair in the living room, holding six-month-old Chloe on my shoulder. She's been very fussy all day and just won't go to sleep. Both she and I have cried a little…

I begin singing to her, and, hearing us, Emma comes running in from the other room and squeezes herself in next to us. I wrap my arm around her. She loves singing all the songs with me. The only problem: when we sing "You are my sunshine" and some of the others, Emma insists on doing all the actions that go along with the words, which of course wakes Chloe up and we have to start all over.

This duet has not been a winner for getting Chloe to sleep…except for when I sing "Lullaby, and good night…"

Emma hasn't created any actions to that one yet. I know the words for only the first two lines, and sing la-la-la for the rest. Which is what Emma does too. She can't say her "l's" yet, so it's "ya-ya-ya", sometimes slightly off key.

So…this fussy Chloe day…"Lullaby and good night…" seems to hold the magic. Emma and I sing it through three or four times. Until Emma tells me, "Softer, Rita." So we barely whisper, singing "la la la…."

After another round, or two, with ya-ya-ya in my right ear, and Chloe's warm breath in my left, Emma tells me, "Stop. That's enough, Rita. Chloe's asleep now."

It's true…

Emma's little hand is pat patting the top of mine. I can feel a tiny heartbeat on either side of me, one against my ribs, the other one, faint on my shoulder.

Chills begin running through my body. The three of us, singing, rocking back and forth, almost as one, being held, in The Great Lap which holds us all.

Never having had children, I had concluded I would never experience moments like this as I grew older. I am overcome. In bliss. ...

"Remember this moment, Rita, remember... and cherish it."

"Why you crying, Rita? ...Are you sad?"

"No honey, I'm not sad at all. I'm...very happy."

"Then why you crying?"

"Well, sometimes big people cry happy tears, Emma."

"Happy Tears?"

"Yes, sometimes big people get happy drops dancing all over inside—

in their hearts... and in little bumps on their arms.

...and pretty soon those happy drops dance all the way up to our eyes,

and come out from the same place sad tears come."

"Oh...Can I have happy tears?"

"Well honey, I'm not sure. I think children have mostly band-aid tears...

or mad 'I-don't-want-to' tears... or sad tears."

"But hey... I want happy tears."

"You will some day, sweetheart, I'm sure you will...

some day..."

"Does Popcorn Come From an Egg?"

We've just popped a bag of popcorn and are happily munching at the kitchen table.

Three year old Emma holds up a huge, white kernel in her fingers, and drops it into the palm of my hand, "Did that come from an egg?"

"That's a great question, Emma. Let me show you something. Let's dig down to the bottom of the bag and see what we find."

I pull out a few unpopped kernels and place one in Emma's palm. "See this, Emma. It's called a kernel. That's what popcorn comes from." *At this point, I don't go into how it grows on ears etc. etc. Too confusing. That can come later, when I will demonstrate with a real ear.*

"A kernel? How does it get to be like that big one?"

"Feel it. It's so hard you could never eat that, could you?"

"Nooooo."

"Well this little kernel is a little wet inside, and when the kernel gets hot—like when we put it in the microwave—it starts doing a little popping dance. Like this."

I begin dancing up and down and puffing hard "hooo hooo hooo…"

"Each kernel gets hotter and hotter and hotter until it can't stand it any more…and then…it POPS open! POP! Into this big piece of popcorn! And then we can eat it."

Emma and I pretend to be kernels, and we do a little popcorn dance together. Puffing and puffing like hot hot kernels about to pop: "hooo hooo hooo…" Out of breath, I sit down on the kitchen bench, rather proud of the new lesson I've taught.

"Yah, yah…but… but does popcorn **really** come from an **egg**?"

A Fire! A Fire!

❧

"A Fire! Rita! There's a fire on top of your head!"

"On top of my head?! Oh no!!"

Ethan's toy sirens are blaring…one fire truck hurries past my shoe laces, up shins, over knees. Up and over every cranny and obstacle a human body can offer.

The other fire truck takes a more circuitous route, criss-crossing hill and dale.

Both trucks arrive at the conflagration barely in time and manage to put the fire out! Whew!

The trip back down winds all around, dangerously, but finally the trucks arrive back at the shoelace fire station.

With all its fiery tangles, my burned noggin will never be the same.

Ethan turns two this month, and the party invitation reads:

"Come to Ethan's Fire House."

Twenty little toddlers! Oh my!

I'm keeping my head out of that one…

    or, maybe I'll just wear a real fire hat that day…

"How Much Is That Dog-gie in the Window? *Arf Arf...*"

⚬

Pushing the double stroller for Ethan and Chloe, my sister Mary and I set off for a walk around the neighborhood. Emma is skipping alongside, holding hands with each of us in turn. It's a nice sunny day, and she has a mission in mind: "Let's look for pets sitting at the windows."

"Okay, let's do that!" Everyone is on high alert. Even Ethan and Chloe, who keep peeking around the side of their stroller. They're into the game too. Every time we spot a dog perched in the window, we stop in front of the house and shout out the old favorite "How much is that dog-gie in the window? *Arf Arf...*"

A few times we also giggle and sing, "How much is that kit-ty in the window? *Meow Meow...*" The doggie/kitty-watch and the singing make for a delightful walk, and we all continue humming and barking even after we park the strollers in the car port and go inside.

As I drive home I'm still singing that song. And even humming the tune hours later as I get ready for bed. You know how a song gets in your head and you can't get it out? Well this one was absolutely relentless. Stuck. Around and around it went.

That night when I wasn't falling asleep right away, I found myself singing it.

And suddenly in the middle of it, I sat bolt upright in bed... barking... in the inimitable manner of that darn song: "*Arf Arf*".

     Out loud. "*Arf. Arf.*"

I looked around to see if anyone else was in my bed that night.

     There was not.

Had anyone in the condo above or next door heard me?

I hope not.

At least no complaints were registered with the manager's office the next day.

I don't know what's become of me...

A Firetruck! A Firetruck!

I find myself seeing the world through children's eyes these days, since I spend a couple of hours with three of them nearly every day. It's a zoo in that little house, a tumultuous world, yet magical, and a magnet to me. My day just doesn't seem as complete as when I've spent some rumble-tumble time in that play-world.

Here's how immersed I've become: A couple of weeks ago, I'm sitting paused for the stoplight at 80th and 15th, when I hear the distant sounds of a fire engine. And suddenly it whizzes past me along 15th. I point and shout excitedly, "A fire truck! A fire truck!"

Then I realize "Oh, I'm alone..." No Ethan. No Emma. No Chloe.

I glance sheepishly around to see if anyone is watching this grey-haired woman jumping up and down as a fire truck whizzes by.

A gentleman waiting for the crossing light has a funny smile on his face, and he is carefully not looking my way. He certainly watched the fire truck go by too. Still, I don't catch his eye as I make my turn at the corner.

I have to smile at myself. I see so much of the world through children's eyes these days, whether I'm with them or not. The boundaries blur.

And then I ask myself: So why feel sheepish about it? It's a good thing. If you think about it, fire trucks really are quite a marvel.

Time to reclaim a sense of wonder at the simplest everyday things.

The Lens

❦

Emma has found a treasure during her trip to the bathroom: an empty toilet paper tube.

"Look Rita, look what I have!" she shouts, peering through the grey cardboard. "It can be a telescope!"

"Shall we pick the white raggedy end pieces off then?" I ask.

"No. It's okay... but now I have to decorate it! Come 'ere!"

We proceed to the living room, where she begins searching through the closet for a special crafts bag. She soon finds it. "Here! Here's some pink polka dots 'n' blue eggs for the telescope. They're supposed to go on our Easter eggs, but it's okay to put 'em on this too."

She glues and she glues, taking her time, choosing just the right colors for each spot on the tube. In between all the gluing, she periodically squints through the emerging telescope: several times at my smiling face. At her favorite stuffed animal Mr. Monkey. At the goldfish crumbs on the floor...

Finally, when she feels finished with her decorating, she turns the tube around and around in her hand, making sure it meets the approval of her artistic eye. Okay, one more dot... there. She looks through it again, surveying the entire living room.

Then, to my surprise, she proudly presents the prize to me. "Here. Take this pretty telescope to your friends. Will they like it?" Her trait of wanting to give things away, to me, and even to my friends, is so endearing.

"Oh yes!" I reply, peering through the small tube to the world beyond, as framed by little white raggedy TP pieces... "I'm sure my friends have never seen anything like it! Didn't they love the sliding board you made from that cardboard piece inside Mommy's shoe?"

For emphasis, and so I'd have something for myself too, she then plasters two tiny blue dots on the front of my T-shirt.

And I am reminded, everything is beautiful—in its own way…

It so depends on the lens I use…

Happy Hour

❧

We've been outside for quite a while in this July weather, watering the garden. The children are having so much fun doing this "task." Everybody's wet of course. When sandbox fun begins, I feel the summer's heat begin to get the better of me. I tell their Mommy, "I'm going inside for a drink of water."

Chloe hears me and comes toddling over. "I go too Ri-a? D'in' wa'wa?"

"Sure honey. Come on." We walk up the steps hand in hand and head to the kitchen. Her clothes are soaking wet, so I put a towel on her booster seat before she climbs in. From the cabinet I take out a little pink plastic glass for her, and a green one for me. She and I spend 15-20 minutes simply sitting at the table drinking our water, having a great time. No snacks. No toys. Just one another and our plastic glasses.

Chloe's learning to drink out of a glass, so we have to celebrate when she is successful at sipping. We do high fives, and clink "Cheers!" with our glasses, and I keep providing her with tiny refills…She plays hide and seek with the buttons on my blouse. She invites her stuffed animals, also present, to sip, and we clink with them too. At one year old, she's already a terrific conversationalist and a born entertainer.

After a while her mommy comes in, a bit worried. She follows the trail of drips into the kitchen, and spots the two of us at the table: "You've been in here a long time. Are you okay? What are you doing?"

"Oh, we're just catching up with one another…"

Before long Emma and Ethan come in too, wanting to join us. They each find their own special glass, and get ready to clink. "Cheers!" we all shout. *I'm touched. Clinking, toasting, has been such a long time family tradition.*

For ten more minutes the four of us simply sit around the table drinking our water, chatting away. Clinking our glasses! Clinking!

After each refill: "Cheers!" all around…time and time again.

It is a Happy Hour indeed.

"Who's In Charge of You?"

My sister Mary, the children's grandma, and I, are driving Emma home after her gymnastics class. At an intersection, suddenly another car whips in front of us and nearly hits us, missing by inches.

"I hate that!" I shout.

From the back seat, Emma scolds: "My mom says you're not supposed to say 'hate.' It's not nice."

She pauses, cogs turning in her mind. Then she continues, still in an admonishing tone of voice: "Who's in charge of you, Rita?"

At first, I don't understand her question. Then I do. She wants to report me! She needs to report this infraction. To someone. An authority. Surely it calls for disciplinary action of some kind.

I wish I had had the presence of mind to say, "When you grow up to be big, no one else is in charge of you anymore. You have to be in charge of yourself."

But in the heat of the moment, I feel the need to respond at Emma's level. Actually, I don't like to hear someone tattling on someone else. But this seems a serious matter.

"Who's in charge of you?" she asks a second time.

With a twinkle in my eye, I glance over at my sister. With some reluctance, I turn to Emma, "I guess Grandma is."

So she leans toward the driver's seat: "Grandma, Rita said 'hate'."

Grandma/Mary: "Rita you shouldn't say that. If you say that again, you might get a Time Out."

Emma leans back in her seat, vindicated, justified. Proud of having done her civic duty.

"Okay, I'll be careful," I mumble.

Later, when it's only my sister and I together, Mary elbows me: "Don't forget. You said it yourself. Out loud. With a credible witness. **I** am in charge of **you**."

I've rued that designation ever since.

Some Questions Are Best Unanswered

Because both parents work, Jeff full-time and Michelle three days a week, they have had to search for part-time nannies, and they have been fortunate to find wonderful young women to care for the children. Most have been in college or graduate school during their nanny months…and after they graduate, they usually move on to more professional positions in their field. They have consistently taken good care of the children, have loved them, and been loved back. What a blessing they are!

One example is Clare. She graduated with a Masters in Counseling, has been away from the family 18 months now, and still the children ask about her. She often comes to their birthday parties and other events.

Shortly after Chloe has moved into a room of her own, she asks her Grandma, "Do you think Clare can come now and have a sleep-over with me?"

Grandma: "Well Chloe, remember, Clare got married, and now she has sleep-overs with her husband."

Chloe: "Well, when she's done with her husband…

thennnn…

can she come and have a sleep-over with **me**?"

Grandma has to turn away, regain her composure.

Chloe is insistent. "So, when she's done with him, can she come and have a sleep-over with **meeeee**?"

Grandma wriggles out of that one. "We'll have to talk to Clare."

I'm All Ears

Following are the results of my latest complete physical, one conducted by four year old Emma. Using the doctor kit she received for Christmas, she performs the examination:

—Listens to my heart with her stethoscope (slightly askew): "Now cough!" I do. ("Mmhmm. That's good.");

—Takes my blood pressure. Wraps band around my arm and pump pumps. Checks the reading: ("2-3-6. That's good");

—Gives me a shot (pokes too hard);

—Applies bandage on my finger (it sags limply);

—Lastly she examines my ears. Using her Princess flashlight and the proper plastic instrument. First one ear, then the other. She runs her fingers slowly all around every inch of the lobes.

Finally, dropping the flashlight, she declares with an air of great authority:

"Well,

your ears…

are…

too **big**."

She pauses, before adding,

"But they're clean. They're very clean."

With that, the "doctor" abruptly leaves the room. Our appointment is over, just like that. No recommendations. No chance to ask any questions. No explanations. Nothing.

I look around…

Grave doubts begin to arise regarding this physician's credibility, her professionalism.

For she has left her instruments strewn all over the floor!

She might actually be a quack.

Regarding my ears?

I am seeking a second opinion.

It's the Police!

❦

It is the happy occasion of Emma's 4th birthday. The invitation reads: "Come to a Fairy Tale Tea Party"...

At one o'clock in the afternoon, right in the middle of the party, there is a firm knock at the front door.

Michelle opens the door, horrified to see two tall policemen standing there. *(Were we singing, "I'm A Little Teapot" too loud for the neighbors?" she wonders.)* The boisterousness inside comes to a complete halt. All eyes stare at the policemen.

"We received an emergency call from this address, Ma'am," one policeman tells her.

The policemen note a tub at the door filled with drinks: juice boxes and bottles of water.

As they peer inside, they see six little pink lacey tables set with tea cups and tea pots. Three and four year olds are running around the room in long ruffley princess dresses and glittery fancy tiaras.

"So sorry, Officers. We did catch our two-year-old son fiddling with the red alarm button. But we thought we'd canceled the call." (But it was from their cell phone, not the land line).

"Without the correct home-phone number listed in the "Cancel," protocol requires that we come immediately to this address."

Again, Michelle apologizes profusely. The boisterousness inside resumes.

She invites the Boys in Blue to come in and share a piece of birthday cake and some juice with us. Top hats or tiaras? They graciously decline, with their apologies.

They do leave smiling… but I wish they'd worn feathery tiaras back out to their car.

Fashionista? *Not*

∽

I wear lots of hats these days. One I have *never* worn is that of "Fashionista." Or trend setter. One of the reasons it's easy going over to the children's: No dress code. No high-style expectations. So I wear my most comfortable, usually some of my oldest, loose fitting duds. No worries.

Until yesterday, when two year old Chloe asks, "Why you wear that yellow shirt again?"

 (What I think she meant was "two days in a row," a phrase not yet in her budding vocabulary.)

I didn't tell her what I was thinking: *Well no one spilled yogurt on it yesterday, or wiped chocolate on my sleeve, or dripped cherry popsicle all down the front of it"—which is why, yes, it's true—Chloe can never wear the same clothes two days in a row. At times there are several changes even in one day!*

"Well," I answer, "because I like it!"

"Ooooh!" she utters with a toddler's pretend understanding. And, then, perhaps sensing she may have hurt my feelings, she adds, "I like the two fishies on your shirt. They're kissing."

There are other moments with the children along this line that warm my heart, ones when I must remind myself: do not take these compliments at face value, given they are merely perspectives and echoed words of three and four year olds.

Once when Emma had just finished combing my thinning graying hair, she put one of her pink barrettes in, and declared: "You look cute."

The next day, again those were her first words when she opened the door:

"You look cute." She must have been practicing for something, I'm not sure what.

Another day, as three year old Ethan and I are just hanging out on the couch, he comments, "I like your shoes." Followed by, "They're pretty." My old shabby dirty Nikes, which I've been wearing over there almost every day for over a year. It's the first compliment Ethan's ever given me. He too must be practicing for some fine day in the future.

Speaking of not being a trend setter, there was one memorable day when, for one brief glorious moment, I was led to believe I might be, at least in someone's eyes:

> I am walking around Green Lake when a woman with her dog stops me.
>
> "Where *ever* did you get that bandana?!" she asks excitedly.
>
> *It's only that classic dark blue bandana, one I had taken to wearing around my neck quite often those days. I had just returned from a trip to South America, where for three weeks it had been an almost daily accessory. The kerchief was a bit faded, though not tattered at all. It felt so comfortable. Even comforting.*
>
> "Oh gosh, I can't remember," I tell her. "I've had it for so long."
>
> "Oh I wish you could remember! I've been looking for one just like that and can't find it anywhere."

I'm pleased—and surprised—that she so likes something I'm wearing. That never happens. I pause for a moment, and then untie the kerchief from around my neck.

"Here," I say, handing it to her. "I've really worn it long enough."

She can't believe it. "Oh thank you!" she exclaims.

But what happens next...I could not believe my eyes! And she does not even have the courtesy to wait until I am out of sight.

Bending down, she ties the kerchief around Benjie's neck! Yes, the dog's. "Here, Benjie! Here's what I've been searching for! Oh my, you look sooooo handsome! It's perfect!"

And with a happy wave, the two of them trot off...

Okay. So much for being convinced, even for a moment...that I might be a trend setter...

Oh well, I'll take a compliment whenever and wherever I can get it...

In any case, I sure *like* seeing the world through the children's eyes!

No wonder I keep going over to that house!

Computer Magic

❧

Emma and I are playing on my computer, when she accidentally hits some key, some something. Everything stops dead. We don't know which key it is, and no matter what I try, the ole MacBook just will not respond. So I stop messing with it. I recognize when a glitch needs professional attention. Tomorrow I will take it over to the Genius Bar at the Apple store.

Without a word, Emma disappears. I think she might just be feeling bad, maybe even guilty, and as 5 year olds are wont to do, is probably moving on to something else to play.

But she returns to my side in a few minutes with an 8 x 11 cardboard sign:

a lovely scene with grass and sun and blue sky. She turns her sign toward the screen and speaks softly, with both an apology and a plea: "I'm sorry. I made this card for you to feel better. Please come back."

It does not.

Undaunted, Emma skips back over to the crafts table and concentrates on her mission. To the original scene, she begins adding colorful butterflies, birds in flight, a laden apple tree, and sweet flowers. Tulips and daisies. Once again she dances over and looks the computer directly in the face with her enhanced get-well card. Her verbal message is also slightly altered: "Computer, I'm sorry I did something to you, but I don't know what I did," she says. "So I made this card to help you get better. It's more beautiful now. Please come back."

Where do such ideas come from in her tiny brain? I am smiling to myself at her magical thinking, her innocence. She is all serious.

The moment she speaks her last word, the computer blinks. Blinks again. (or winks??!)

Presto! The screen flashes back on! Brings up the original page.

To **my** absolute utter amazement,

but not to hers.

Emma dances with joy.

Forget about the Apple Genius Bar.

WHEN SOMEONE
IS HURTING

Band-Aid

At the children's house this morning, I nicked my finger and it began to bleed a bit.

Little two-year-old Chloe sees it, and asks, "I get a Band-Aid, Rita?"

She jumps down from the couch and runs in to the nearby bathroom closet. Points out three boxes, though she can't reach them. "You want a princess Band-Aid, a Pirate, or a Racing Car?"

I choose the Pirate.

She instructs me, "Wash your finger first." She reaches on tiptoe to pump a huge squirt of soap onto my finger. "Rub it in good, Rita."

She grabs some toilet paper to dry it since "you don't want to get blood on a towel".

Bits of TP stick to my finger at first.

Chloe helps me tear off the wrapper, and puts on the Band-Aid, though a bit lopsidedly. All the while she is assuring me: "It'll go away, Rita. It'll get better."

Of course she needs one for herself too. We examine her arms and her legs, and can't quite find any owie. Finally she decides to have it on her arm, same place as mine.

And then the two Band Aids have to kiss. "It'll get better…"

This is not the first time I've worn a character Band-Aid.

When Emma was about the same age, she had a similar reaction.

I had scratched my arm in the car on the way over to her house.

"You need a Band-Aid," Emma's mom, says to me, examining my arm. I can't find the adult ones though. Will a Dora one be all right?"

"Of course. Thanks," I say.

"Dory Dory Dory!" shrieks toddler Emma at the sight.

D-D-D-Dora. She has a Dora phone, a Dora Jacket, a Dora Tee, and takes her Dora books into bed with her for nite-nite.

Standing on one leg, leaning against the couch, Emma watches closely as her mommy carefully places the band-aid over my "owie".

Seconds later, she whimpers a little, holds her arm up, pointing to the same place.

"Do you want a Dora Band-aid too?" her mommy asks.

"Yah."

"Don't you still have the one we put on your knee a while ago? Oh, all right."

A minute later, Emma boasts a Band-Aid twin on her arm. Her mommy and I kiss it.

Even Elmo and Mr. Monkey kiss it, and the Dora phone comes over to kiss too. Emma is satisfied, and comforted. We all feel better.

Emma and Chloe are learning lots of things, especially the seeds of empathy: hurting when someone else does. They learn that human beings gather around a person when she or he is hurting. They are learning to be kind and to do what they can to help ease the hurt. They get their turn too.

Lavender Brushing

Is it possible for a 2 ½ year-old and her mommy to have a big misunderstanding?

I wouldn't have thought so until yesterday, when an unfortunate happening occurred just as I arrived. Mommy (my niece) comes to the door to let me in, carrying one-year-old Ethan. Toddler Emma is hopping up and down just inches away. She's holding a metal matchbox car in her hand, and in her exuberance to see me, she flings it high up into the air.

When it comes down, the metal car lands squarely on her mommy's toe. Mommy shrieks with the sudden unexpected pain, and tears come to her eyes.

I take Ethan from Michelle. She drags Emma toward the Time Out Room.

"You don't throw things at anyone!" As Emma disappears into time out, she turns toward me with a puzzled, frightened expression on her face.

From Time Out I can hear Emma repeating, "I sorry Mommy. I sorry."

Meantime, Ethan is squirming in my arms, wide-eyed and worried-looking.

After Michelle's foot is propped up, and she is applying ice to her toe,

I seize the moment to describe what I witnessed.

"You mean she didn't actually throw the car at me?"

"Not at all. It went straight up."

Mommy hobbles across the living room in to Emma. Soon the two of them emerge, tears still lingering in their eyes.

We had intended to go for a walk, but Mommy's toe is too sore when she tries to get into a shoe. Just Emma and I head over to Green Lake, with me pushing her in the little red car.

We chat with crows and seagulls, myriad doggies. We stop to pick up some pine cones, pretty leaves, and assorted sticks. We are on the path only about 10-15 minutes when Emma looks at me, "Need go home. Mommy. Mommy."

Never is this active toddler ready to leave the lake. Never before has she initiated a return, never wanted to head toward home, even when we've been gone an hour or two. Or three. But this day it is clear that something is weighing on her little mind. My hunch is that she's never seen her mommy cry.

"Mommy. Mommy."

We turn toward home.

As we walk down the alley toward her house, we pause to pick three sprigs of lavender from a bush behind one of the neighbor's garages. Emma clutches them tightly.

I begin to coach her, "When we go in the door now, give these to Mommy. They'll make her toe feel better." I am not sure she understands. Usually, after sniffing and sniffing lavender, she begins tearing it apart, and treats it like some kind of science project.

But this time, the very minute we step inside, Emma thrusts the bouquet of lavender toward her mommy. Michelle holds it up to her nose. "Oh, Emma. They are so pretty and they smell wonderful.

Thank you, sweetheart." Michelle places one in her top blouse button, "so I can smell it" and leans back, putting her feet up on the ottoman… leaving the other sprigs on the coffee table.

Emma picks up the two sprigs and begins lightly brushing her mommy's toe with it. (It is not even on the injured foot, but that seems not to matter at all, to anyone.)

Slowly slowly, back and forth, back and forth this little girl brushes. "…make Mommy toe feel better…make Mommy toe feel better…"

In that moment some unspoken hard feelings soften between the two of them.

All is forgiven, on both sides.

Lavender is known for its healing qualities.

So are toddlers.

Reunion

I've had pneumonia. It's been two weeks since I've been with the children. I just can't stand not seeing them any longer. Making sure it is a time when meds are not making me drowsy, I ever so slowly and ever so cautiously, drive myself over to their house. I've missed them so much. I tear up when I arrive. They give me such excited welcomes: "Rita! Rita!" I can't even get my coat off before the hugging begins.

The children are so different in their welcoming, each reflecting their unique personality:

Emma grabs my attention immediately, excited to share her news: "We've got roses, Rita! The roses are out! Come 'ere! Come 'ere!" She pulls me outside around to the back to show me. And there they are, red red roses hanging over the carport. We take a few minutes to smell them, to marvel at their beauty.

When we go back in, **Chloe** comes toddling over and throws her arms around my legs. "Ria. Ria." Little arms reach up, "up uppa" and we have to cuddle and cuddle so tight. She does not let me slip her off my lap the whole time I am there. The two girls just stay close to me, hugging and engaging me in every way. We read "Purplicious," and we look through the treasures in their pink polka dot purses...miniature books, pieces from puzzles, shiny wrappers from chocolate treats, paper hearts, tiny stuffed animals, and even some stale cheddar goldfish.

And I find myself believing more and more in "nature" as well as "nurture" re how boys and girls are different. Because when two-year-old **Ethan** saw me coming through the door, he came grinning and shouting running over toward me...but stopped short, about a foot away. I tousled his hair, and hugged him. He reached out for my keys with the floating bubbly stars keychain. "Is the pink key a triangle or a pentagon?"

Today he wants no part of cuddling, but he keeps shouting over from a few yards away as he is playing with his mini-cars: "Rita Rita!" And I call back "Ethan Ethan!"

"Do you want a yellow car, Rita?"

"I'd love one!" So he runs over with one yellow car, rolls it along my thigh and parks it there. Same with tiny "garbage truck" and "dump truck" that vroom across my shoe, up my shins, and around my knobby knees…until I have a thigh-full fleet of his toys tooting their horns:

Hey, I love you too, I missed you too!

I return home soooo happy, though tired too.

Being with these children—such good medicine.

Purple Toe TLC

On my way to the condo luncheon, I hurt my big toe—smashing it under the heavy iron door when I swing it open too swiftly. I scream and cuss a bit. I can barely hobble.

The next day, when I venture over to the children's, I explain to them what happened.

I carefully put my foot up on the large ottoman in their living room. But with all their running around, my smashed toe keeps getting bumped, and I yelp more than once. So to remind themselves to be more careful, they build a tent of pillows all around my foot for protection.

I tell the three that my toe will turn purple, and they are ever so curious. They want to know "How purple?" "Will the whole toe turn purple or just right where it hurts?" "Does purple hurt more than pink?"

So, when I come back the next week, and the foot is much less sensitive, I ask, "Do you want to see my purple toe?"

"Yes!" they shout. And gather around.

Ever so slowly—partly because my toe still hurts quite a bit—I remove my shoe, (no drum rolls) and then… slowly… slowly pull my sock off.

Speechless, the three simply stare at the injury for a moment. Then…

Emma reaches for a soft red blanket and wraps it around me, giving me a few pat-pats.

Chloe says, "I'll put a pillow behind your back." She picks up an orange one from the couch nearby, and carefully tucks it behind me. She keeps calling me "my little Rita," perhaps because she senses my vulnerability at this time. She continues with "my precious lovely Rita, my best friend..." Lastly she animates my little stuffed animal Skippy to sing a love song to me, that she makes up as she goes: "Oh Rita Rita I love you love you... toe get better...don't be purple, don't be hurt..."

Without a word, Ethan runs out to the kitchen and returns with an ice pack, which he gingerly leans on my foot, frowning at the problem of how to secure it on my toe. "It won't stay on," he says. Chloe knows what to do, and disappears for a moment. "Here's Huggy Bear to hold the ice on your toe."

"Good idea, Chloe! Your bear can make it stay there." And he places the little valentine bear face-down over the ice pack.

Miracle Worker

I have had two total knee replacements, with long scars to show for it. Each time the children ask me to get down on the floor with them, I remind them that it hurts my knees too much. And I show them the scars.

Three-year-old Chloe has always shown great curiosity around those scars. Sometimes when I'm wearing shorts, she traces her index finger ever so lightly over each knee.

One morning when it's just she and I together, she comes over to me holding a bottle of hand lotion, saying, "Rita, pull up your pants here." She's tugging on the left pant leg.

She helps me pull the hem up so my scar is showing.

Chloe proceeds to massage my knee with the lotion. Ever so tenderly she massages and massages, then runs for a Kleenex, and wipes off the excess. "So it won't get on your clothes."

She follows the identical procedure for my second knee. I am amazed at her staying power. And I'm touched as well.

"Thank you, Chloe. My knees feel so much better now."

She grins at the success of her efforts.

"Now…" she pleads, "…now… ??

can you get down on the floor and play with me?"

Whatever Works

Emma is at preschool, and little Chloe is napping, so it's the rare occasion when just Ethan and I have time together. He includes me more in his play when it's just the two of us....

As I'm walking across the living room, I stumble on a tiny Lego piece, turning my ankle a bit and almost falling. Luckily I am facing the couch, and I pitch forward onto its softness.

"Ooooooooh" I moan, putting my face in my hands.

Hearing me, Ethan immediately comes over and puts a necklace over my head—one he has been using to hook his train together. (Before I stepped on the Lego, I had been marveling at his ingenuity: engaging one of Emma's big-bead necklaces in service for that purpose.)

He decides that the train-necklace is not enough to comfort me. So he motors over five of his mini cars, one at a time, and sets them on the couch, right next to my leg. Lastly, he runs in to his room and returns with Pooh Bear, his favorite stuffed animal. He places Pooh on my lap.

"There."

All this without uttering another word.

But the caring of this little boy speaks volumes.

Ethan always likes to keep his favorite playthings close by; they make him feel good.

He figures they will do the same for me.

And you know what? They do!

Pause...

Even when I'm on the computer
    I often pause between words
        for half an hour or so...
not filling pages with revisions,
      or alternatives
Rather, opening my small world to the world
    beyond words.

I simply pause,
    let streams of sunlight pour in
      like they already were
        before I noticed.
Whitecaps are whitecapping
    like they were
      before I glanced up.

Now if it should come to pass,
    that the brilliant sun is beaming in
      and I just keep my head down
        and keep on typing away...

I hope someone's there to call me on it

      my kitty, my spirit, my writing buddy,

        someone to shake me…

          awake

So that I will sit up

    stand up

      kneel down

whatever it takes to remember

   to honor to marvel

      to be present

        to be still

          to be…

Then I'll go out and blow bubbles

   in the wind.

SHOWING KINDNESS

A Catalog of Kindnesses

Emma was given a "Kindness Award" at pre-K this month! We are all excited and proud of her. We celebrate with ice cream and cake and talk about Emma's kind acts that her teacher had observed.

Then, we discuss some other possibilities for practicing kindness, such as praising how Emma jumped down from her chair to pick up the pen that Chloe had dropped. And we talk about what's **not kind,** like hiding something that someone else might like or be looking for...

To begin giving this kind of recognition at home, I start a practice of counting the children's acts of kindness. They'd ask: "Is this one?" Literally counting, they'd ask "Do I have six now?"

It was all about getting the children into the habit and helping them recognize what is kind. With a little coaching, lots of compliments and encouragement and even reporting their kindnesses to their parents—for more attention and praise—the children seemed to be getting the idea.

We also began pointing out and praising other people's acts of kindness when we noticed them.

One particular morning Ethan is intent on practicing. "Chloe," he says, "I like your pony tails."

"Thank you Ethan."

"Wow! That's five kindnesses for you," I exclaim.

But Chloe, after waiting a moment, corrects him, "They are braids. Not ponytails. So do you like my braids?" Her brother is noncommittal on that one.

When Emma comes home from Pre-K, we report that Ethan committed nine kind acts while she was gone. She is curious, and asks, "What were they? What did he do?"

Here's what we remembered:

1. He told Chloe "I like your pony tails!"

2. He asked Chloe: "Did you paint this?"

"Yes," she said.

 "It's pretty."

"Thank you, Ethan"

3. "I like the brown owls."

"Thank you Ethan."

4. In Zingo, he let Chloe put the heart chip on her card even though he needed one on his, too.

5. In Slapjack, Ethan hid the "Halloween Cat" because it scares Chloe.

6. When I was changing Chloe, I didn't know where her diapers were.

 "I'll show you!" he said. And he did.

7. When he was hungry and wanted a snack, I told him I would get it for him after Chloe fell asleep. He was patient, and said, "okay."

8. He picked up all the magnet pieces, even though he was not the one who had gotten them out, nor had he played with them at all.

9. He wiped the crumbs off of Chloe's chair before she sat down.

"That's really good, Ethan!" Emma exclaims.

Mark one down for Emma.

"Take This Home With You!"

I don't know how this practice got started. Even at two and three, Emma always wants to give something to us as we are leaving. Something of hers.

"Here, take this with you." "Take this to your home" or "…to Mukilteo" or "Take this to your work" to Daddy or Mommy. Or "Take these to your friends." It might be one of her flowers from the tiny pink vase up on the mantle (that I fill nearly every time I come).

Or a craft project. Maybe a favorite sticker…

I cannot walk out the door without carrying something tangible from her in my hand.

One day though, she gave me a flower that was almost dead. So we had a talk about that. "When you like someone, you give them something nice, something you would want to have." After that she became insistent on giving one of her favorite flowers, or maybe even her last one: A huge red tulip, so wide open with such a beautiful pattern in the middle. Or two wee daffies. Sometimes it's just a pink petal that she places gently in my hand. Always I accept gratefully…

Every time I leave, Emma asks, "Why are you leaving?"

"Can't you stay some longer?"

"Where are you going?"

This day I explain: "I'm going to stop by to see some friends who are moving away."

From her tiny vase she chooses two lavender sprigs and a red daisy. "Here, take these with you. Give them to your moving friends."

So I did. And they appreciated the posy as much as I…

Taking Turns: Skippy Comes For a Visit

Ethan meets me at the door each time I arrive, looking for the special bag I carry for all the stuff I bring to their house. "Can I find Skippy? Can I have Skippy?"

Skippy is the little stuffed puppy who rides around with me in my car, and often comes in to visit the children and their menagerie. "Okay. See if you can find him."

Ethan digs deep in my six-compartment bag (it's really a wine bottle carrier, free at the QFC, when you buy six bottles). Skippy's doghouse is one of the six pockets.

"Here he is! Here he is! Hi Skippy!" Ethan exclaims. He pulls Skippy out and runs to his little sister. "Here Chloe. Here. Here's Skippy."

Ethan and Chloe used to fight over who got to play with him first, and Skippy would barely escape with his life. If the children got rough with him, then the next time they'd ask, "Where's Skippy?" I'd say, "Well he's staying in the car. He didn't want to come in to play with you today, because he hurt his tail here last time."

But that has become rare. These days, though Ethan always makes certain that he pulls the puppy out first, he knows that Chloe loves Skippy so much that he gives him to her to play with first. This pleases them both, and me, too.

Each time Skippy has a play-date at their house, he is given royal treatment. He's under Chloe's care much of the time. She hugs and kisses him. Hugs and kisses him. Then takes him in to visit her own stuffed animals. "Skippy's here!" she announces to them. They'll gather around, one at a time, to greet him. Hello Kitty always pays a visit, as does Fuzzy Wuzzy, Curly 1 and Curly 3.

When Emma gets her turn, she usually dances and twirls with Skippy or has him do flips in the air and other gymnastic tricks. Ethan invites him over to the long windowsill to marvel at his Lego masterpieces. Dutifully, Skippy hops up and down, excited with it all.

One day he lost an eye during his visit. After an intense hunt, Ethan finds that little dot on the floor! In a group surgical procedure, we glue it back. Then for several hours Skippy has to recuperate out of reach, up on the mantel in the living room, where he is visited, blown kisses at a distance, and offered "candy" to make him feel better.

When it's time for Skippy and me to leave, the children's stuffed animals gather around to give Skippy a group hug. His little head is usually poking out of his cubicle as he and I go out the door. He waves his paw shouting, "I love coming to your house! I love you! See you later!"

The Microphone Tree*

I would have walked right past those little treasures; in fact I had already, numerous times. I had even crunched them underfoot, without a thought.

Today Emma notices them. Lying right there on the sidewalk, not even an inch long. She stops in her tracks, "Look, Rita, baby microphones!" She picks up one tiny stem, holds it up to her lips, and immediately begins singing into the tiny "mike" while dancing around, right next to the busy street.

She picks up another, and handing it to me, says, "Here, Rita. This one's for you!" So I start singing into it and dancing too, right next to the busy street.

Before we walk on around the block, she picks up several more. "One for Grandma…"

she says, then leaves one on the top step for Molly, her favorite neighborhood dog. "Here Molly, you can bark loud now."

When we get back to the house, I remind her, "I have to leave soon, honey."

"Why?"

"To go to school, to write."

"With your writing friends?"

"Yep."

"What do they look like? Are they nice?"

"Umhmmm."

She pauses a moment before asking, "Would they like to have a baby microphone?"

"Why yes, I think they would."

So we put our coats on again, and walk the half block from her house to the magic tree. One by one, Emma tucks about 20 "mikes" into her baggie. "Here, give these to your friends. Is this enough?"

"Yes, Emma, everyone can have one now! Thank you!"

My writing friends really get into the spirit of it, and as class ends, they sing "Happy Birthday" to me, holding the new toy mike up to their lips…

My poem that day reads:

"We each have one: An invisible microphone.

To sing into,

whatever song is ours alone to

sing,

our voices carrying far above

the tallest branches of every tree."

"Are You Okay?"

It's a warm sunny day as Emma and I begin our walk around the block. Before we set out, Emma picks some bluebells and some dandelions from her yard. She collects some wildflowers from the alley as well. "I'm going to give these to people we see on our walk," she confides. It becomes her sole purpose in this walk to give something away, to make people happy. She's never done that before. And I don't know what inspired her. I am touched.

The first person we see is a man working in his front yard. "Here's a flower for you," she says and hands him a dandelion, just what he's trying to get rid of. But he rises to the occasion saying, "Why thank you!"

As we walk along, we don't meet many other people, so she begins laying a flower here, or sometimes a couple of camellia petals there, in the middle of the third or fourth step. "Won't they wonder where a bluebell came from? It will be a surprise!" she beams. Silent gifts.

Just as we are about to turn the corner heading back toward her house, we spy a man across the street just going up his second set of steps, almost at his front door. As we cross the street, Emma is shouting to him, "Wait. Wait. I have a flower for you!" I note that he is elderly, and call to Emma to let him go on into his house.

At the same time, I'm not looking where I'm going, and suddenly find my toe hitting the curb. I go stumbling, stumbling forward, and land flat on my stomach. Luckily, not on the sidewalk, but in the grass. I look up to see Emma on the sixth step, almost to the man, though the man himself is looking down at me with a horrified expression on his face. He begins descending the steps again, very slowly, and so does Emma, not understanding what has happened.

She's puzzled, if not hurt, that the man does not receive her flower, or pay any attention to her.

I get myself up to a standing position sooner than I feel ready, so the neighbor won't have to help me, as he looks quite old and frail. I am almost erect as he arrives at my side, and he touches my elbow, though I make certain he has no weight to bear.

The elderly gentleman is speaking quickly, in Chinese, I believe, nodding, with a concerned look on his face, checking to see if I am all right. I keep assuring him that I am.

"Emma now you can give him your flower." So she presents him with her bluebell. He smiles and bows, smiles and bows, then proceeds back up the steps holding his bluebell.

"What was he saying? Did he like my flower?"

"Oh yes. But at first he didn't see your flower because he was worried when he saw me fall," I explain. "He was not speaking in a way that you and I do. Later, when you gave him the bluebell, he liked it a lot."

As Emma and I walk on, I tell her, "When you see someone fall down, it's nice if you go over and ask, 'Are you okay?' and try to help them up, if you're big enough. It makes them feel better."

"But I didn't see you fall down, Rita. I just saw you sitting on the ground."

"Oh honey, yes! Of course! You were walking up the steps when I fell, weren't you! I'm sorry!" *I feel chagrined, realizing the truth of her words.*

Holding hands, we walk on a few more steps. Suddenly she stops, looks up at me, and asks softly, "Are you okay *now*?"

Counting Kindnesses

As I come in the door, Ethan asks, "Did you bring your Dinosaur Birthday Party cards with you, Rita?" He loves this game of concentration, finding pairs that match.

He digs into my bag, finds the set, and begins laying them out in rows of four in the middle of the living room floor.

Then he disappears.

Two minutes later he returns, dragging a white kitchen chair behind him. "Here, Rita, now you can sit with us and play." He realizes that there's no sitting place nearby, and knows that I can't get down on the floor.

By then the other two have gathered around, and Emma is feverishly making dinosaur matches. Ethan also finds two matches and places them in front of his little sister. He finds two more and lays them down in front of me. He keeps none for himself, not concerned about getting his share. By that time Emma has claimed all the rest.

Ethan claps and shouts, "Emma is the winner!"

Later we all go outside into the sunshine to play. Chloe falls and scrapes her knee and it is bleeding and she is crying. Without a word, Ethan disappears again, and soon runs back carrying the butterfly ice pack. "Here Chloe. This will make your knee feel better."

Back inside, he asks, "Rita, are you counting kindnesses today?"

"Yes, honey, I always do. You have ten!"

"I think Emma and Chloe have ten too," he replies.

Behind My Pillow

Just behind my pillow as I hum myself awake each morning
Just behind my pillow...

    reside gifts of the dawning day...

        waiting...to tap me on the shoulder.
I breathe life in...gaze out at the early sky.
Let's see. Today's Friday.

I close my eyes again.
Each planned event presents itself in living color...
Appointments...a walk along Shilshole with a dear friend...
playtime with the children,

    watching kindness come alive...

        How will the day unfold...

          and how will I?

      How can the arms of one single day hold so much life,

        so much that is dear to my heart!

And then...Every night, as I lay my head down

    on the soft pillow of my day,

        the reel of those waking hours replays itself,

on the clear magic screen behind my eyelids.
The happenings return...one by one...
most, anticipated in the morning—
some surprise encounters too.

I grin a lot, and often laugh out loud, there on my night pillow.
Tears are known to appear as well.

Time set aside for pondering, and gazing at the shimmering water.
A few questions arise...not so much asking how did I do:
(was I kind, was I present in the moment...)
though that's woven into my review...

Mostly I simply marvel—isn't life just a kick!
and to think I'll get to live it another day!
(Well...I'm not positive, though the odds are pretty good.
I'm counting on it!)

Tomorrow—oh tomorrow!

Okay, it's time to turn off the reel...
file it away...

go to sleep now

on the soft pillow of today

to be ready for the morrow...

its unknown gifts

aquiver

in the wings of my dreams.

THE WORLD OF FEELINGS

"I'm Sorry"

❧

Three-year-old Emma is back in her room in Time-Out, where she has been sent for scratching me. *(Yes, on purpose)*. After three minutes, her Mommy calls in: "Okay, you can come out now, Emma, if you're ready to say 'I'm sorry' to Rita."

"I'm –not- talking."

Silence.

"I'm not talking!"

Silence.

"I'm not talking!"

"Okay, you can come out when you're talking again, and

when you're ready to say 'I'm sorry to Rita."

A few minutes elapse…

Soon Emma begins sauntering ever so slowly out of her room over to the kitchen table. She sidles over toward me, pauses about a foot away, at the jumping jack, where her baby sister is playing. She reaches down and turns the ABC's music on. As the song begins, she looks directly at me and sings, ABCDEFGHI'mSorryLMNOP."

It's like saying you're sorry without having to say you're sorry.

A singing apology couched in the ABC's. Hey, that counts for me.

"Well thank you Emma for singing 'I'm sorry'.

It's not easy to say I'm sorry, is it?"

"No, it's hard."

"Want to know something? It's not easy, even for big tall people. Like Mommy or Daddy or Grandma or Rita."

She just looks at me. "It's not?"

"Unh-unh. But you know what?"

"What?"

"Everybody feels better after someone says I'm sorry. Even the one who says "I'm sorry" feels better. And then it's over with."

She hops up on my lap and we go on with our day. I don't know how much has sunk in.

As I'm driving home, I begin pondering how this has happened, that even at three, it's become difficult to say "I'm sorry." Three seems so young for this. I didn't know it started so early…

What is the root of this great reluctance, I wonder. In this family, we do not label a child "bad" or shame her in any way, but simply let her know when behavior is unacceptable.

I'd like to figure it out. Psychologists talk about "pride." Or shame or guilt. I think it could involve something else. A child comes in to this world as a being of all- goodness, and for months and months knows nothing different. She is perfect.

When the first "no" comes, I can imagine she is stunned. How can this be? I am perfect. How can anything I do be "wrong"? or "How can someone I love be hurt by something I do?" It is utterly incomprehensible. Some innate sense of her own goodness may be thrown off balance.

This may also be part of a child's early process, I'm not sure.

Adult modeling is helpful in this dynamic. Some parents think it is not appropriate for adults to apologize to children. Not true! It softens the relationships…

I've heard Mommy say to the children: "I was really grouchy today. I'm sorry."

I've heard Daddy apologize to the children, and Grandma as well.

As have I. I think of an instance not long ago: One afternoon I gave Chloe some gardening gloves I'd given Emma a couple of years before, but which she had outgrown. Emma became really upset, and shouted, "Those are my gloves! You should have asked permission from me first!"

She was so right! And I felt bad. Apologized. And then asked permission. Which Emma granted.

And all was forgiven. We could be friends again.

"Are You Happy?"

❧

Just as I am about to pull out from the curb this afternoon, my niece Michelle comes running down the sidewalk, flagging me down. She's carrying three-year-old Emma, tear-streaked and barefoot, (knowing if she'd taken time to put shoes and socks on I would have been gone).

Puzzled, I roll down the window.

"Emma's upset because she didn't get to give you big hugs and kisses before you left."

"Well honey, I'm sorry. Just jump into the car a minute."

Emma climbs over and squeezes herself in between the steering wheel and me, straddling my legs. She holds on tighter and longer than usual.

She leans back and looks at me, "Are you happy, Ri-ta?"

"Yes, I am very happy. You make me happy, Emma. Your hugs and kisses make me happy. Thank you for coming way out here to give them to me!"

Mommy and Emma are scrambling back to the house as I drive off.

❀

"Are you happy, Ri-ta?" Emma asks me that nearly every time I am with her. Out of the blue seemingly—in the middle of playing cards, or munching on a taco, or walking in the park. She asks it of her Mom and Dad and Grandma too. No one knows where that question came from. It often serves as a bellwether to me though.

Less frequently, she asks, "Are you sad, Ri-ta?" or "Are you mad, Ri-ta?"

Usually that's around something specific that she's done, like sprinkling milk or water all over the counter; or knocking her little brother down.

But most of the time, it's "Are you happy, Ri-ta?"

As I drive off I am reminded of a story John Lennon told:

> *"When I was 5 years old, my mother always told me that happiness was the key to life. One day in school, they asked me what I wanted to be when I grew up. I wrote "happy".*
>
> *They told me I didn't understand the assignment.*
>
> *I told them they didn't understand my answer."*

I think Emma might echo John's words some day. I sure do.

"Where Is My Fam-i-ly?"

Grandma (my sister) has invited the little family up to her condo for Thanksgiving.

The inside of her condo is spacious, and just around the corner on her floor is the "Party Room" which she had reserved ten months ago for this occasion.

Mary's computer room becomes the play room when the children are there, and she keeps on hand a whole trunk full of toys that they see only when they are in Mukilteo with her.

Ethan loves this room, these toys, especially the cars whose wheels come off. He is totally engrossed in playing, and seemingly pays no attention to the conversations and goings on in the nearby kitchen and living room. At some point, his Mommy and Grandma and his two sisters leave to begin carrying decorations and plates over to the party room.

Suddenly the condo is silent.

Ethan stands up, looks around, and says to me, anxiously, "Where is my fam-i-ly?"

"They're just down the hall, Ethan."

It's not like we're in the mall or lost in a maze or something.

Again he asks, "Where is my fam-i-ly?"

He doesn't just say, "Where is Mommy?" or "Where is Daddy?"

"Okay, honey, take my hand now, and we'll go find your family."

All the way down the hall he repeats, in the most wistful, plaintive voice, "Where is my fam-i-ly? Where is my fam-i-ly?"

We turn the corner, and there we can see into the Party Room, for the walls are all glass.

Suddenly he catches sight of his beloveds, and his mood swiftly shifts. He shouts, "**There** is my fam-i-ly! There they are!"

He lets go of my hand, and dashes into the room as fast as his little three-year-old legs can carry him: "My fam-ily! My fam-ily!"

His mom sweeps him up in her arms and hugs him.

Puzzled

"I don't want Rita to come in!"

I am stunned by Emma's words today as I appear in the doorway.

She usually greets me so warmly. Not today. She continues screaming: "No, I don't want you to come in. No, I don't want Rita."

At her mom's insistence, I finally let myself all the way in anyhow, in spite of Emma's protests. She immediately pushes Ethan down, so Mommy puts Emma in time out. Screams grow even louder.

When Emma emerges, her mommy takes her directly out to the kitchen for lunch, as she has refused anything to eat all day. Maybe she's just hungry. Meanwhile, I am in the living room feeding Chloe. Emma doesn't come in to see us as she usually does. It is a weird time …

A little later in the day, Emma gets mad at me when I scold her for hitting Ethan. It's been a tough day for her. "You can't come to my birthday party!" she shouts at me.

"Well that would make me sad," doesn't seem to melt her resolve.

So I add, "And you know, you might not have any balloons at the party then, because I'm the balloon lady."

She ponders that unthinkable possibility for the briefest of moments.

"Okay, you can come."

After dinner I kiss everybody good-bye, and leave, still puzzled about the morning's reception.

What I can't believe is how hurt I really was. By this little three year old. Shows me how much I really have given her my heart.

Her mommy reassures me, "You belong to the club now. Emma has acted like that to all of us."

Well so I joined the club today. But it doesn't feel good at all.

"God in My Heart"

The setting: The children's parents are meeting with new home-owners out at the kitchen table. It's after 9 p.m., and I am putting 2 year old Chloe and 3 year old Ethan to bed. Their bedroom is upstairs, on the same floor where the kitchen meeting is taking place. Emma's bedroom is downstairs, and I've promised her I'll return in twenty minutes or so to tuck her in too.

Ethan interrupts me as I am reading "Fireman Dan" to him. "Emma's crying. I can hear her." We both stop to listen, but I can't hear that sound. "Emma's crying," he repeats in his soft little voice. "I'll go down soon," I assure him.

I read Chloe's chosen book to her too, and then head back downstairs. A tiny figure is sitting at the edge of the couch, slumped over, not just crying, but sobbing, sobbing.

Hmmmm. So Ethan really did hear her.

He has followed me down the steps. "Why are you crying, Emma?" he asks.

Sobbing, wiping her tears…she tells us:

> "Because I am lonely … down here
>
>> all by myself
>>
>>> I am lonely…(she pauses…)
>
> But…
>
>> but God is here in my heart."
>>
>>> (she pats her tiny heart.)
>
> and … I don't feel so lonely …
>
> But still, I am lonely."

Hmmmmm. This little girl could make a believer out of me.

I'd like to get to know a god like hers. "A personal God" I think believers say. It's true. I'd like to know a god like that.

> *I used to. I think I used to...*

This feels like Emma's first poem:

> **God in My Heart**
>
> **I was feeling lonely down here**
>   **all by myself.**
> **But God was in my heart.**
>   **and I didn't feel so lonely**
>   **any more.**
>
> **But still,**
>   **I was lonely.**
>
> *~Emma, 2014*

Upset

꧁

At last, it is time! This weekend has been declared **The One** when the family will finally be able to move from their seven month stay in cramped quarters downstairs—to the remodeled three bedrooms upstairs. I'm on hand hopefully to keep the children from getting underfoot during all the hustle and bustle that's sure to go along with that undertaking.

It has been a tough several months, as remodeling often is, since the family moved into their new house. Tempers have flared more than once, especially as the end seemed in sight. Patience is running thin. When I arrive late morning, it has already been a challenging day. Mommy has taken all three to swimming classes as well as on her trip to Costco, while Daddy has been working non-stop on getting the rooms ready upstairs. Cleaning cleaning. Laundry, laundry. Lunch, Lunch. A flurry of activity.

The children and I are putting some puzzles together downstairs, when we hear angry voices upstairs.

"Mommy and Daddy sound mad," Emma says softly.

"Well, I think they are upset."

"Why? Are they mad at me?" she wonders.

"No. Oh no, honey. They can't find something they really need in order for everybody to sleep in the new bedrooms tonight. They're hunting all over."

"Ohhh."

It's the last straw for the parents. They cannot locate the hardware for the beds they'd taken apart when they moved from their Green Lake home. In today's search they have removed dozens of boxes from the huge Storage Container parked in the front yard, as well as from the indoor storage room and the garage, opening each of the boxes, searching searching for the missing hardware. All these boxes now sit in the front yard, and will have to be re-packed before nightfall.

Such a seemingly tiny glitch is able to hold up the entire move! It interferes with the anticipated joy of the day. The parents are utterly frustrated. Exhausted. Become curt with one another. They can barely hold it together. "Mommy and Daddy sound mad…"

Meanwhile, what do the children learn? That it can't always be peaceful in their house. Or fun. Or perfect. That Mommy and Daddy do get mad at one another.

"But you know what?" I tell them. "You have heard Mommy and Daddy get angry before, haven't you?"

"Yah."

"Well, do you remember? Once they finish being mad, things usually calm back down again, don't they?"

"Yah."

Feelings Can Change in a Flash

Mary and I have been taking care of the three children for five days, night and day, at her condo, while the parents are working every spare minute getting their new home ready. It has been very challenging. This fifth evening all three have been bathed and are in their jammies, teeth brushed. My sister Mary calls them together so she can read to them in her "Magic Bed" that goes up and down.

Chloe pushes Emma away, "I don't want you to sit next to me." None of Mary's pleading helps.

Now this might have been a teachable moment…I didn't know if a behavior of Emma's had precipitated Chloe's response. But my sister and I were too ragged to explore.

Our patience had run thin by that time of night. I step in to the bedroom, thinking some kind of intervention might be called for. Mary welcomes it.

"Emma, why don't you come out to the living room with me, and we'll play on the computer." So she does. She is still sobbing at her little sister's rejection.

"Can you make me a card, Rita? Tell me you hope I feel better soon."

She's often amazing at knowing what she needs at any given time. And articulating it.

"Sure. I'm really sad that Chloe hurt your feelings, honey. And I do hope you'll feel better soon. So let's write that down."

Emma snuggles up close to me on the couch, leaning over to see the words I am typing.

She is pleased that she can read almost every one as I type it. Very slowly, one letter at a time, I write: **Dear Emma, I hope you will feel better soon. I love you. from Rita**

"Shall we put some pictures on your card, some of your favorite things?"

She doesn't hesitate. "Yah. A heart."

I click on Google "images" and enter the word "heart." Emma is amazed at all the hearts that appear, and finally chooses a green one, which I drag over to her card.

We follow the same procedure with:

      A butterfly   A flower   A snowman

"We can print this off now, Emma, and you'll have my card to take with you."

      Her reply takes my breath away, her level of self-awareness,

        of emotions moving in and out:

"Okay, but first take off the part 'I hope you will feel better soon.' You don't need to say that. Because I already do. Just have the pictures on it and "I love you."

This card, slightly rain-splattered, rests atop her dresser in the new house.

"I'm Scared"

Emma is going to a different school this year. I find her crying. "I'm scared to go to Kindergarten. I won't know anybody there."

"Yah that's hard, honey. But you know, you've done a lot of things you were scared to do, and you found out you could do them just fine. Remember? Like when you started pre-K."

"Yah."

"When you think about going to a new school, and feel scared, take a deep breath! Like this."

Imitating me, she takes a deep breath.

"Yes, just like that. Then you can say, "I'm scared AND I know I can do it.' That's called having confidence in yourself."

So she says, "I'm scared AND I know I can do it."

"So if you catch yourself fretting about going to Kindergarten, you can say

'I'm taking a deep breath. I know I can do it.'

Then you can take another deep breath, and go back to playing or to coloring or whatever you are doing."

Later we are playing "Kitty Kitty" downstairs. She directs me to be the kitty, and she's the mommy.

So I start crying, meowing.

She runs over to me, with this assurance: "It's all right. Mommy will be with you. She will be right there to pick you up when Kindergarten is over."

This little girl is learning that she has the power to control her own thoughts.

It's a lesson that took me a long time to understand, to realize. As an adult, it took a lot of practice in shifting my thoughts, in order to change the way I talked to myself.

The secret was in catching myself in the moment when it was happening. Shift…shift…

A deep breath always helps…

We believe what we tell ourselves.

And we can change it…

Love Is in the Air

Lately, nearly every day when I arrive, Emma begins crafting a heart message that has my name on it, which she can now spell. Always hearts, usually rainbows, clouds, sun, flowers, and grass. Proudly she presents the art piece to me before I leave. One day when I'm there she draws everything in sparkly ink. When I hug her and say, "You're my favorite five year old in the whole world!" she quickly calls on her new skill to count by tens. Stops when she gets to 80, and says, "And you're my favorite 80 year old!" Then counts by 5's to 80! Then teases me and counts to 100. "You are 100!"

The same day, little Chloe is feeling sick, so she and I cuddle and rock a while in the nursery. "Read me a story." She chooses "The Kissing Hand": about a little raccoon who doesn't want to leave her mommy to go to school.

"I have a secret," the mommy says. "Hold out your hand."

Mommy kisses the palm of her little one. "See it in there? Any time you're missing me, just hold your hand up to your cheek and feel my kiss. It's always there."

Chloe and I practice this before going on with the story. She likes that game a lot.

Ethan has joined us for the story,

but wants nothing to do with the kissing part…

*The story continues: As the little raccoon leaves for school the next day, she tells her mommy, "Now **you** hold out **your** hand." And this time the little one kisses her mommy's hand.*

Chloe and I practice that one too. (But not Ethan).

Always as I am leaving, there are Hugs, Hugs all around. Then it's such a delight to see three little heads watching out the window as I walk down the steps and climb into my car. Remembering the story, Chloe presses hand to cheek. Hand to cheek. Ethan grins and waves. Emma points to herself, draws a heart in the air, and points to me. I return the air heart and all their greetings. Then as a final goodbye, I wave out from my open sunroof as I'm pulling away...

Often tears fill my eyes as I am driving home, warm-cheeked. Love at the window, love in Emma's papery heart crinkling in my pocket, love in the tiny green alien someone tucked into my purse, love wrapping itself all around me.

Enveloped in a circle of Love. Love. Love is in the air.

"Invisible threads are the strongest ties." ~ Friedrich Nietzsche

OUT AND ABOUT

Dandelion Pillow

༄

Emma has become very interested in little creatures. Not spiders or flies that come inside, but outside ones. Today it was snails. First she decides to draw one at the kitchen table, and I am quite surprised at the accuracy of her sketch. "How do you do that?"

"I just notice shapes," she explains.

A little later she and I go out into the yard, where, as luck would have it, she spots a snail on the front sidewalk. She lifts it up so gently and carries it out to the back "where no one will hurt it." She picks a dandelion and puts it right next to the shell "so it will have a pillow." Then she pulls some blades of grass and breaks them up in tinier pieces "so it'll be easier to eat."

Finally, she places a circle of bluebells around the little creature "so it will be protected."

(I am astonished at this procedure...)

The next morning he was gone. I had cautioned her about that possibility...

"Do you think he got cold last night? Do you think he could sleep better with the pillow?

Was he happy?"

"I'm sure he loved his pillow, and that he slept better, honey. But when he woke up this morning, he had things to do...and just had to get going..."

"Weeds Are Flowers Too ... once you get to know them." ~ A.A. Milne

It's February by the time Emma and I get out for a walk for the first time this winter. She notices how everything is so brown and dead—the microphone tree, all the flowers: the hydrangea, the tiny roses bushes, in their "jackets" (Emma's word) to protect where the buds are waiting to come out. In the alley she notices the hollyhock stubs, the bare cherry blossom tree, and the vines where grapes used to hang down over the fence.

We also spot tiny crocuses coming up everywhere. We say hello to the tulip leaves just beginning to appear. "I hope they are pink. But if they are not, I will like their color. Are there rainbow-colored tulips? That would be best."

As we round the curve into the alley, she spots the clump where dandelions always come up. Emma stops in her tracks. "Dandelion buds Rita, two dandelion buds!" she yells excitedly.

"The dandelions are coming up! They're my favorite! They are sooo yellow."

She just has to pick them. She hides them behind her back before presenting them to her Mom, who properly oohs and ahhs. Emma places them in her little pink vase on the mantle. "Maybe they'll open up!"

To make a fuss about something so mundane, usually quite detested by adults, so yellow!

I want to revive that kind of excitement for the ordinary things in my own life. For the typically not-wanted things.

I want to see them differently...as if for the first time.

Falling in Love With Her Shadow

∞

She's falling in love with her shadow.

"Wave to your shadow!"

   She does, and the shadow waves back.

   She stands at the wall, entranced.

Here's someone that will do everything she tells it to!

She's learning to be a big sister,

   more affectionate than jealous

   more sharing than possessive…

               (though not *all* the time…)

She's falling in love with the ABC's

   and with words too, hundreds of them,

      um-brel-la, gro-cer-ies, ep-i-sode, el-e-phant, ot-to-man.

She can spell her name, real fast.

   She counts everything, and names them first: birds on the
telephone wire,

      dogs we pass along Green Lake,

         every step she walks up—or down.

She can sing now, really carry a tune. When did that happen?

   And she loves all the songs:

"Rain, rain, go away,

    come again some other day."

      "Frere Jacque, Frere Jacque…"

      "Twinkle twinkle little star…"

      "Itsy bitsy spider…"

She's especially fallen in love with books.

Some get to spend all night with her,

    and nap-time too.

  "I just yooooove books."

      She puts herself to sleep "reading" one

        out loud. Very loud.

With all the expressiveness in the world.

"I just yoooooove _____."

Fill in the blanks. She "yoooves" everything.

I've fallen in love with her shadow too,

      and even with mine…

    and it's like I'm learning the ABC's

    all over again,

The ABC's of life, of what matters.

We're both falling in love with this world…

Moonstruck

❧

How does a child learn what is real and what is not?

This question arises Halloween evening, as I'm in the company of a 2 ½ -year-old monkey and a one-year-old tiger. With their Mommy and their Grandma (ages yet to be revealed), we've trick and treated over at U. Village Halloween event, and then stopped for pizza. When we exit the pizza parlor, I ask, "What if Emma and I walk home? It's only three blocks."

Mommy says okay.

Toddler Emma looks all around. She has never before gone for a walk at night.

"It's dark."

"It is. But can you see me?"

"Yeah."

"I can see you too. We'll hold hands and stay real close to one another. Okay?"

"Okay."

"See all the street lights out there?"

"Yeah."

"They'll help us see where we're going."

"Okay."

We set off, and in the shadows she's not so shy anymore, and becomes the bold monkey inside her suit. "EE-EE Ah-ah…." She takes huge bouncy monkey steps, longer than my stride.

We come into an open space. "Oh, look up in the sky, Emma! It's the moon."

Crescent and clear it shines.

She stops in her tracks. "The moon!?"

"The moon!" she shouts. We take a few steps and she stops, staring up again. "Moon. Moon."

She walks unsteadily a bit, not watching where she's going, unable to take her eyes off the magical sight.

The moon—there really is one?

What is real and what is not?

"Where the stars?" One of her favorite books is "Goodnight, Moon." In all her books, stars always accompany the moon.

"Tonight we can't see any real close to the moon. But look! Lean your head way back against me. See those tiny points of light high high up there? Those are stars, Emma."

I hold her shoulders as she leans back and gazes upwards in wonder. "Stars! Stars!"

A few minutes later, we come to a man standing at the bottom of a long set of steps, recruiting trick-or-treaters. "Please go up and get some treats," he urges. "My wife is waiting with some just inside the door up there."

"Oh, I wish we could," I tell him, "but I'm sorry, with my knees, it's not safe for me to go up and down those steps without a railing, especially holding a little hand."

"Well could you wait here just a minute and I'll run up and ask her to come down."

So he does. And we do.

The woman hurries down the steps to us, carrying a big bowl of candies. She stoops down to Emma, puts her arm around her, and begins talking to her. About monkeys, night-time, tasty treats.

Meanwhile, above their heads, her husband is mouthing the words "Thank you" to me.

Emma chooses her candies, and some for me too. With a "Thank you!" and "Bye-bye. See you later" we continue on our way. The couple trudges back up the steps, the man with his arm around his wife, their voices gladdening the night air.

I wonder about their story. Is she ill? Did they want children and have none? Or had they had a child, and something tragic happened? Or just lonely? Just kind? I don't know.

Soon Emma and I arrive at a busy intersection, with no stop sign or traffic light. It is, though, well lit by a street light. Four teens are standing close by. Seeing us pause at the crosswalk curb, one boy hurries over, grabs the lime-green safety flag from the telephone pole holder, and steps out onto the street to stop traffic for us. Hippity hoppity Monkey and her hobbly grey haired pal hip-hop across, waving thanks to the stopped cars. One honks back.

Once across the street, we wave back to the teen guard, and find ourselves on Emma's very own familiar block. Jack-o-lanterns beam out from nearly every porch. We have to pause a moment and stand in front of each one, marveling, while noticing the unique details in each.

"Oh, that one has silly eyes!"

"That one has only two teeth!"

Finally we're almost back to her house, when the family's car lights start flashing on and off, on and off, to show us the way, to welcome us home.

So Mommy's been tracking us, waiting in the car...

As I'm driving home, I ponder once again: *How does a child learn what is real and what is not?*

I think: From a night like tonight.

Happy Blooms

Emma comes running in to the children's play place at McDonald's shouting "Happy Birthday, Rita! Here!" She's carrying a huge gorgeous pink cyclamen which she thrusts toward me and plunks down on the table in front of me. I love this plant that appears late each fall, brightening up the season with its colorful display.

"Dark pink. Hardy" the label reads.

However, this one seems to be not so hardy, in fact, a bit worse for the wear. Not exactly dilapidated. But depleted, for sure. One whole side has been ravaged. Lots of empty "stalks" poking up.

Ethan and Chloe come running in right after Emma, proudly holding aloft the cards they've made. "Happy Birthday, Rita!" We're celebrating my 80th.

Their parents follow closely, heads down, looking apologetic. Their 2, 3, and 4 year olds had been busy with this gorgeous plant in their midst—on the twenty minute drive between when church ended—and 12:15 when they jumped out of the van at McDonald's!

"What did you do to Rita's pretty flowers?" Daddy scolds.

"Picked 'em," they proudly declare. "For Rita!"

And why not?! It's the most natural thing. And actually, I myself may be to blame. After all, I helped Emma plant gardens in the back yard last spring. And when the hundreds of flowers came up so profusely, well what did we do? Picked 'em. Nearly every day of the summer. Put them in Emma's little pink vase up on the mantle.

I suspect that these children have never laid eyes on a houseplant before. No respectable, intelligent one would dare appear within 50 feet of their house, for obvious reasons. It wouldn't have a chance.

The three children enjoy Happy Meals, in between shouting and laughing and high fives for sliding down the long winding slide. Then everybody sings "Happy Birthday" while downing hot fudge sundaes…

Just as we are driving off, Mommy pops her head out from the van, waving pink detached somewhat forlorn cyclamen blossoms and petals she'd found strewn about on the back floor of the van.

"Want these?" she laughs. She tosses them merrily up into the air, their pink upswept petals fluttering off in happy birthday breezes.

This poor bedraggled cyclamen now holds a place of honor in my living room. It was and is one of my favorite birthday gifts. The naked stems speak to me of the children's touch, and that is precious. I can see their little hands perched like blooms at the top of the shriveled stems. Happy blooms of a different order.

Just yesterday I happen to spy, safely buried deep down, hidden in the dark green patterned leaves, a few tiny buds that had, quivering I'm sure, narrowly escaped the keen eyes and itchy fingers of six busy little hands with nothing else to do while riding in their van for twenty minutes—except pick pretty pink flowers to give their Gr'auntie Rita on her 80th birthday.

Sam the Moth

❧

The three children and I are out in the back yard playing, and simultaneously weeding one of the garden beds. Emma happens to see "a creature" (as she calls it) clinging to the wall nearby. "What is that?" she asks.

"It's a moth."

"What's a moth?"

"Well it's kinda like a butterfly, like a cousin, but it's not colorful, or beautiful like a butterfly. Lots of people don't like to have them around."

"They don't? Well I do." She plays a while longer, then returns to it.

"Why isn't it moving? Flying around? It's just been staying real still on the wall for a long time."

"Look closely, Emma. Part of one wing has been torn off. It can't fly any more."

"It can't fly?"

"No, honey."

"It looks so lonely just sitting there on the wall. No friends or anything. Do you think I can help it?"

"Well I don't know. You can try."

Ever so gently she lifts the moth from the wall and cradles it in the palm of her hand. Lightly pets it. The moth seems not to object.

When she lays the moth on the sidewalk, it can barely walk. A couple of legs are missing.

"Is it a boy or a girl?"

"It's hard to tell."

"Well I'll call him 'Sam'."

"What do moths like to eat?" she asks.

"I'm not sure." *I dare not say "Cashmere sweaters."*

Emma spends the next hours relating to Sam, creating a safe and charming shelter for her new charge. "So he can have a home, and a family. Since he can't fly back to his own family."

She commissions Ethan and Chloe to collect some long green leaves, and some little pink flowers. Two yellow day lilies too. They obey her orders. She finds a hefty stick, and with the leaves, she builds a little lean-to that Sam crawls under. She fills a tiny seashell with water. She surrounds it all with a circle of day lilies and greens, and constructs little bridges and ramps made of sand and sticks and long flower stems. She leaves a space in the circle "a door so Sam can go out for a walk if he feels like it."

He decides to, but fails to use the specified exit, just climbs up and over a pink flower. Emma gasps when she sees him heading toward a huge crack in the cement, one that his whole body could easily fall through. Hurriedly she constructs a little bridge of sand and sticks. Ooops he veers away from the bridge! So she simply lifts him over the chasm. He walks only a few more feet, and then stops. Rests. And does not move for a long time.

She confides in me, "I think he's dying…"

After a while Emma lifts him back over to her refuge. Every so often, she bends down to within an inch of Sam, and whispers some re-assuring words, encouraging him. "You're safe now" and "I'm staying here so you won't be by yourself". "I like you even if you're not pretty like a butterfly."

Next to the lean-to she winds a tiny circle nest of dried brown grass. At the end of the day she gently places Sam in it. This time, so he won't be exposed out in the sidewalk circle, she places the nest in a separate little container under the steps, complete with one tiny flower and the water-filled seashell. Across the top she spreads large green leaves one at a time. Leaving spaces "so Sam can breathe", but hiding him "so a crow can't kill him…" and "so he won't get wet if it rains."

The next afternoon when she returns home from school, there is no sign of Sam, and pieces of his refuge are strewn everywhere. She begins searching frantically all around the yard. "Where is he? What happened to him?"

She considers several possibilities, none of which she will accept. What she finally concludes: "Sam's parents found him! They were happy he had been protected, and taken care of, but they wanted him to come home. So they carried him back there."

"Do you think he liked the home I made for him?"

"Oh yes. I'm sure you made him happy, honey. No one likes to be alone when they are dying. It means so much if someone takes care of them, makes them feel special."

Later that day, when we are practicing her reading, I ask, "Would you like to write a story about Sam, Emma?"

She declines. "No it makes me too sad. The way it ends."

"Well honey, sometimes it helps to write the sad stories too."

TOGETHER, WE LEARN

Emma Stands Her Ground

When Emma was in pre-school, she became the target of another girl's bullying. At school, at gymnastics, even in her own house. The two girls had lots of play dates together, and over time had become "friends." So were the Moms.

I witnessed the unkind behavior more than once. For example, I watched, through the viewing window during a gymnastics session, how Emma became frenzied, like a frightened rabbit, running, running. Every minute focused on B, who was teasing her, taunting her the whole time. B slapped the big ball out of Emma's hands, hit Emma with the ball too. On purpose. Knocked her off the bars, behind the teacher's back. That made Emma angry. Me too.

At Emma's own 5th birthday party, B. gathered three other girls around her in a circle but would not let Emma in, saying: "I don't like your clothes." "I don't like your toys."

During the party she held hands with Chloe and Ethan, but would not with Emma.

As the months passed, Emma's mood began changing drastically. She often became sullen and sad. She balked at getting ready in the mornings, crying: "I don't want to go to school. I don't want to go to school…" She began to misbehave, to sit it out at parties or social events when B was present. Her overall confidence waned.

Once after a particularly rough gymnastics class, Emma and B were scheduled for a play date at Emma's house. However, when B and mom arrive, Emma is standing at the doorway of her house clutching her nanny's hand tightly. She says: " I don't want you to come into my house. I don't want to play with you."

Emma holds her ground, with the nanny's firm support. B and her Mom turn around and return to their car.

"I don't know whether B is going to be nice to me, or mean," Emma confides.

After that, Emma and I have a talk about trust, and what it means when you can trust someone. And how she wants to act in ways so that she can be trusted too…

The moms decide the girls need a break from one another, so they do not get together for several weeks. However, when they resume the play dates, B's unkind behavior continues.

Finally, the moms decide they must sever the connection altogether, agreeing:

"B and Emma are not at their best selves when they are together."

Emma's mommy was willing to sacrifice an important friendship of her own for her daughter's well-being…

It was not easy.

Tomorrow, Tomorrow...

When Chloe was a little baby, she had a most unusual way of crying. Her cries literally went up and down octaves, many decibels filling the house.

Even at six months, I kept telling her, "You're going to be an opera singer."

Now two years old, this little girl sings night and day, and in tune. She knows the words by heart (even if she doesn't understand them) to ten or fifteen songs, and sings in her inimitable toddler tongue.

One afternoon Chloe and I are playing on her magic slate. She's drawing circles, which I'm turning into snow people. Suddenly she bursts into song, one of her favorites:

"Tomorrow, tomorrow,

I love ya, tomorrow

You're only a day away."

We keep drawing snow people while she is singing. Suddenly she stops all the action. "Erase," she says.

Which she does, swiftly. With great deliberation, she pulls the sliding bar across to expose a brand new clean slate.

"Tomorrow. Rita. What is tomorrow? Can you draw me a picture of tomorrow here? What tomorrow look like?"

Hmmmmm. What do I say?

"Well honey, after you go to bed, when you wake up, tomorrow becomes today."???

Not to a two year old.

What if we do with our tomorrows, what Chloe did on her Magic Slate. What if each morning we erase at least the negatives of the day before—all the anxieties, failings, the regrets—and open up a new page, a new slate. "Today is a new day!"

We can do that…for that's the way each new day dawns… brand new.

"Life hangs by such a slender thread." Now is all we have.

Oh, and back to Chloe's question… Well, it was time for me to leave then.

"I have to think about it some more, honey. How to draw it. Maybe tomorrow…"

Two Neighbors

Emma and I are walking down the alley on a warm afternoon. The first neighbor we meet is not friendly.

"This is Emma," I say, smiling.

"Yes I know Emma. Hello, Emma." Not the hint of a smile.

I tell her, "I usually let Emma pick a sprig of lavender or two out here in the alley. I hope that's all right."

"The bees can sting you," she warns. "And the lavender is being pulled up from its roots…"

I realize she had heard us coming and has stepped out to confront us.

Emma is sad. Me too. We do not pick any lavender from that spot again, and in our walks we simply pass by the purple springs that line the fence in the alley behind that house. I buy Emma her own plant and we find the perfect spot for it in her back yard.

A week or two later, one of the highlights of our walk is meeting Mr. Don, owner of the big white house at the end of the block. He is in his driveway, putting stuff in the trunk of his car as we stroll by, and we say hello.

Mr. Don is so friendly, asks Emma her name, and mine too. I tell him how each day when we walk by we always admire the hollyhocks growing right at his sidewalk.

He is surprised. "Oh, is that what you call those?" There is only one left. "Would you like this red one, Emma?"

She nods. He reaches into his trunk for scissors, and cuts it for her. She grins, with a shy thank you.

"And look back there in my yard. There are lots more. Pink ones. You can come and pick those any time you want. There are raspberries back there too, golden ones and red ones. Pick anything you want."

He goes on: "I'm not home very much, because I'm taking care of my Mom who's 95. She lives only a few blocks away. Today I'm putting new insulation in her house."

We thank him and continue on. "That's a nice man," says Emma.

We each leave legacies, even in such small ways. Every time Emma and I walk past that empty stalk, Emma remembers, and says, "Here's where that nice man cut his red hollyhock for me." And sometimes we find golden raspberries too.

Mirror, Mirror, on the Wall

Everything has its beauty, but not everyone sees it. ~ Confucius

❦

She is combing my hair. Combing, combing, oh so gently. "Why is your hair so short?"

"Oh it's so easy to take care of that way."

"Take care of? You need to take care of your hair? Like have someone stay with it?"

I realize she's thinking "like nanny-care."

"Oh, combing my hair and brushing it and washing it is taking care of it."

"Oh."

Emma keeps on combing…combing my thinning gray hair…

Her next comment, without preface, stops me in my tracks. Catches me off guard.

"I am more beautiful than you are."

I take a deep breath.

I wish I'd reacted swiftly enough to ask why she thinks that. What does a 4 ¾ year old child know about "old", about society's prejudices? Does she think wrinkles are ugly? or grey hair? or that my clothes aren't pretty? I don't know.

Instead I say, "That's not a very nice thing to say, Emma. To me, or to your friends or to any body. It might hurt someone's feelings."

She keeps combing my short hair, a little more slowly now…

"You **are** beautiful, Emma," I assure her. "…And so am I. But I am not more beautiful than you are. And you are not more beautiful than I am. Everyone is beautiful. Do you know why?"

"Why?"

"Because God made everyone."

"Oh."

"Can you guess what makes people more beautiful?"

"What?"

"When people are kind, they are more beautiful. But when people say mean things, they aren't so beautiful right then."

Without another word, Emma drops the comb and runs off to the other room.

Did any of my words sink in? I don't know. My hunch is I may have said too much, too much for a four year old to take in all at once.

I think it won't be long though, before Emma begins to glimpse the many ways of being kind. It may take a while longer though, for her to see what makes someone truly beautiful.

It's Okay to Be Okay

It's supposed to turn cold this mid-November night. So while it is still light, Emma and I go outside and sweep up leaves to protect and cover her flowerbeds. She is a real trooper, spreading leaves over the plants with her trowel and garden gloves...

Suddenly she poses this question: "Is everybody good at something, Rita?"

"Yes," I tell her. "Like you, you're a terrific gardener. And a wonderful big sister. Not everybody gets to be a big sister, you know. And you draw fun pictures...

"Yes, everybody's good at something. But nobody can be good at everything. It's okay to be okay. Just so you do your best. And have fun doing it."

She pursues this no further with me. I realize that Emma's question comes on the heels of comparisons being made by the unkind girl at gymnastics. This girl is more adept, more graceful, even more seasoned—and she takes every opportunity to rub it in and rub it in, often making fun of Emma's valiant attempts...

After twenty minutes or so, when I believe we are finished, Emma wonders, "Hey what about there where my tulips and crocuses are? Do they need some leaves or something over them?"

"Well honey, being deep down in the dirt will protect them."

Nevertheless, she begins pulling up grass to put over where we had dug holes and planted bulbs a few weeks before.

She is very happy, pleased with herself when she finishes: "My flowers will be really warm tonight when it gets so cold, won't they!"

Yes, Emma is a good little gardener. She is adept and graceful with her plants, careful and tender with them.

Beyond okay.

Highest, Biggest, Fastest, Kindest

❧

At four, Emma begins exhibiting a worrisome habit: comparing herself many times a day to everyone—especially to her little 2 ½ year-old brother and her one-year-old sister. If an adult is complimenting the prowess of one of her sibs, she interjects: "But I can jump highest." "I'm the biggest." I can run fastest." "Am I the tallest? the fastest? the best ___?" And she's become quite bossy, using an almost angry tone of voice. Constant comparisons, even in magazines. "Am I bigger than that girl?"

I don't know if that's typical of four year olds or not.

Emma and I begin having some conversations about how comparisons make other people feel. And I've given her a few hints about what she might say instead, that would make them happy, like "Oh you can jump so high" or "You can really run fast."

After lots of repeats, it hasn't seemed to sink in.

Until…

One day while we are in the living room playing, I hear Emma say, "Chloe, you can jump higher than me!" After which Emma looks shyly over at me to see if I have noticed. I give her a big smile and an encouraging nod. That is a good first try.

Later on when she and I are walking around the block, I tell her, "You're getting to be such a kind big sister. You made Chloe happy today when you told her she could jump higher than you. But, honey, you want what you say to be true. It's easier if you don't say anything about yourself when you're complimenting someone. Just say something about what they're doing."

That doesn't seem to sink in either…or so I believe…

In the last week of summer our nanny Clare drives the three children over to my place. The first thing they spot is the set of swings on the grounds. They all dart over to them, Emma in the big one, and the other two in the snug toddler swings.

Emma asks me to give her a little push to get started, and then she wants to be on her own. She has learned to pump, and is so proud. Clare is gently pushing the other two, alternating her hands.

From my perch on the bench close by I shout: "Wow! Emma! You are going so high!

And look at Chloe and Ethan fly!"

A few minutes later, out of the blue, Emma calls out at the top of her lungs, "Ethan, you're going so high! High as a **giant**!"

Ethan starts giggling and giggling. Chanting to himself, "…high as a giant, high as a giant.."

Emma turns to me, so serious. "Why is he laughing, Rita?"

"Because you made him so happy when you told him he's going high as a giant!"

The whispered aside, *"But I'm really going highest, huh Rita?"*

"Yeah. That's our secret."

Emma beams all the more. And pumps her legs. Pumps.

Still swinging high, she shouts again, "Ethan you're going higher than a giraffe!"

More giggling.

"Higher than a giraffe sitting on top of a giant!"

Giggling, giggling, all three.

Me too, giggling.

Mingled with tears welling up…

Touched by the rare privilege of bearing witness
to tender buds of goodness as they begin to open
in a little girl's heart.

"If You Ever Want to See Me Again..."

One early August day Emma cautions me…"If you ever want to see me again after I start Kindergarten, it has to be on Saturday afternoon or Sunday afternoon. But sometimes I'll be at a birthday party then…or something else…"

Even the summer weeks are filled. On Monday she has gymnastics; Tuesday ballet, Wed. Art class. Thursday: All sports. Friday ?? Sat. swimming

She recites many possible obstacles to our spending time together like we have been.

"That would really make me sad, honey.""

"You could get a picture of me instead," she suggests.

"Do you think I'd be satisfied with just that?!"

She shakes her head, with a shy grin.

Overhearing our conversation, Mommy chimes in from the kitchen: "Oh, I know Rita. She will find a way for the two of you to have some time together."

Emma jumps right in: "So can you come have a sleep-over with me tonight?"

Tonight? She's free tonight! I grab this chance.

"I Am Reading!"

❧

Emma is in a new school this year. All the other kindergarteners have been together for two years working on phonics and other skills, and Emma confides sadly, "The other kids can read, but I can't." Her parents buy some flashcards and a set of Bob books.

Before they tuck Emma into bed at night, they do their best to work with her. But by that time of night, everyone's tired. Emma gets frustrated and impatient with herself. The parents too. Hearing this, I offer to work with Emma, adding, "You know, I've taught hundreds of kids how to read."

The parents accept my offer in a heartbeat. Emma is skeptical. Until I tell her too: "I used to be a teacher. I taught first grade."

"You diiiiiid?"

"Yes, and I taught 2nd grade too!"

She is impressed. My stature soars! I am now legit.

Three o'clock on Wednesdays becomes our standing reading date. First we work on new "sight" words from the flashcards. We struggle reading the Bob books. Short vowel sounds. "Mit…and…Meg…t-uuu-ggg on a rrr-aaa-ggg." *(Gag…)*

"What does that mean? What is a rag?"

As I think about it, I've never seen a rag in their house. This modern age.

There are: Sanitary wipes.   Feather dusters   Mr. Clean "erasers"   Swiffers   Microfiber Dusting Cloths

      But no rags. Which I just happen to have in great abundance.

So the next day I take over a show and tell: A piece of my raggedy, holes-all-over red T-Shirt. I tell Emma, "Pull on it now, and I will too." And thus she begins to understand "…tug on a rag."

Still, this is not using everyday kinds of words; it's not the way she talks. Nor are Mit and Meg names of people she knows. This does not classify in her mind as "reading."

So I change my tactics, and begin placing flash cards across her bed to make real-life sentences. Creating flash-card names of real people she knows, like "Mommy" and "Daddy". Now that she loves! "More More!" she begs, for the first time ever.

"You-can-go-before-I-do." "Now let's read it real smooth."

And she does.

After dinner she pleads to go at it again. And then, "Can we take these words upstairs and show Mommy and Daddy?" So we do.

We spread across the bench two sentences made of flash cards, and I call for everybody's attention. "Emma wants to show you something. Please listen."

They all turn toward Emma—Mommy, Daddy, Chloe, Ethan.

Emma begins reading the flash-card sentences, proudly and confidently:

"Mommy- said -I –can- go."

"Can- you –come- with –me- today?"

She grins her huge grin, and we all clap, shouting "Good job!"

With that, in cheerleader fashion, almost dancing, Emma flashes each word toward them, one at a time. She shouts:

"Can!

  you!

    come!

      with!

        me!

          today!"

Suddenly she gasps. Her eyes open wide in sudden realization. She shouts: **"I am reading! I am reading!"**

Mommy, Daddy, Ethan, and Chloe all stand and applaud some more. A standing ovation! We all begin dancing around with Emma. Who's twirling in delight.

   She doesn't cry for joy.

   But I do.

Try, Try Again

On this warm sunny March day, the three children and I are out playing in the yard, with Mommy close by, when we happen to spy a tiny snail on the front steps, trying to make it up to the top. We watch and watch the little creature. He has to defy gravity when he reaches the lip of each step, where he clings almost upside down. Several times he falls back down, rests a while, and starts up again.

Mommy says, "Try, try again."

A few minutes later, when the snail falls back down, Emma repeats her mom's words, "Try, try again."

The snail keeps at it. And now it's a chorus of us all: "Try, try again."

While we are watching this process, Mommy says to the threesome, "That's what we all have to do too. Keep trying…"

At one point we spot a little brown thing behind it. Is it a foot? No! The little snail leaves the bit behind. "I think that's poop!" shouts Emma. "The snail pooped!" And she was right!

When she finds that I can't answer all of her questions, Emma asks, "Can you get a book about snails for me?"

I do. It is fascinating for all of us…

Which brings us to decide to find a pet snail, a creature billed as "being a great first-time pet for children. It is interesting to watch and very easy to care for…"

Now that is another story.

Screen Time, Our Time

⚮

The blinds are drawn when I step inside today, and the living room is all dark. I'm surprised. After all, it's the middle of the day and sunny out.

With the TV screen backdrop, I can discern three little silhouettes, but it's as if the children themselves are not there. As if I am not there. No one comes over to hug me. Not Emma, not Ethan, not Chloe. They are only silhouettes. Motionless.

"Hi everybody!" I say cheerily. The nanny waves to me from her perch on the carpet. But no child looks up, or responds in any way. An episode on TV grips their attention: "Paws Patrol."

All three seem unaware of my entry, my presence. Unaware of anything that's happening around them, so immersed in the screen are they. I truly believe they do not hear my greeting, or hear me speak at all. That truth alone concerns me deeply.

I know in my heart that they value our playtime, and I do, too, immeasurably. So I remind myself, "Don't take this personally," — especially since this wonderful household is careful to limit screen time, careful to monitor the ways they allow their children to participate in activities. I realize that even with their iPads, it is a double-edged sword: the children need to become computer fluent, yet so much that is crucial in a developing mind happens away from screens.

I join them on the couch for a while, lightly touching each one. "I can't see now!" Ethan informs me. So I carefully scrunch over out of his way.

Today my time with them is limited, and I must leave before the episode is finished.

"I have to go now," I explain, tousling the hair of each one. "I love you! See you tomorrow!" But I am speaking to the air. All is silent, once again. Still…

The nanny waves her good-bye to me.

As I am closing the door, I pause to glance back a moment at the three silhouettes. What did they see today instead of a Gr'auntie who loves them and loves to play with them?…

Was I merely a silhouette to them too? What was lost?

I walk slowly out to my car, feeling a strange heaviness, a sadness even. At this moment I feel disconnected from these precious children, acutely so, since we are used to being really connected when we are together. It's a huge void. I wonder: Do they even know I was there? Was I? After a while, a part of me had seemed to drift away…

❁

This scenario plays out so rarely at the children's that I found myself unprepared today… And after all is said and done, Emma and Ethan and Chloe will walk away from these early lives so closely connected to mine…

They will have searches of their own, struggles and joys and pain that they probably will not share even with those closest to them…

Today was just a taste…

REFLECTIONS

"Am I Old?"

"Am I old?" Emma asks me.

"Well, you are six years *old*. When you are born, we talk a lot about "how old" you are. Like we say, "She's six weeks old." or "She's five months old."

"But I mean, am I *old*—like you?"

"Well, honey, that's different. It's easy to count 1 2 3 4 5 6 to how old you are. Since I am 82, you have to count a long way to get up to that number." She starts counting, and runs out of breath.

"See what I mean? That's soooo many years, and that's what old old is. I am one of the lucky ones (at least that's how I feel right now…) who gets to live a long time. Not everyone gets to …"

Each day I find myself increasingly aware of the meaning of these "bonus years" and I appreciate their value all the more. I enjoy my old age. I cannot remember the last time I was bored. I laugh a lot. Am easily brought to tears as well. Live so simply. I presume very little … and I take nothing for granted these days. I would not ask for anything more … I am grateful, grateful beyond the telling.

Realizing that life can change in an instant, I am acutely conscious of living in the great unknown. All the more must I develop qualities necessary to tolerate the uncertainty that comes with these years. I must create ways to keep fears at bay—fears like that of becoming dependent, fear of Alzheimer's, fear of becoming rigid in my ways, inflexible, and cranky. I can feel the tension in my body when I start going in that direction, and I don't like it at all.

I've discovered that what often tends to throw me into a fearful state is when I am confronted with some aspect of my aging. And then if I deny it. Denying some aspect of neediness, of dependency, evidence of my body deteriorating, I get defensive. "I'm fine."

I remember a time not long ago when I was with my sister Mary, walking with our brother along the Mississippi River, on a path designed for both pedestrians and bicyclists. There was not room enough to walk three abreast, so I strolled slightly ahead of the other two. When a biker behind us would ring his bell to pass, Mary would shout, "Move over, Rita! Here comes a bike!" As if I couldn't hear the bell.

Well, the truth was, I often could not. Though I was adamant in stating that I could. Later that day she reminded me about things like "Remember to use the bathroom before we leave the house." I became more and more irritable. The two of us distanced ourselves from one another.

That evening the tension remained between us, and I did not feel good about being unkind to my sister. I told her, "I realize what you do is out of caring; I know that with a certainty. You may have to do such things for me some day (she's eleven years younger than I) but I'm not there yet, though at times I feel I'm getting close." We agreed on some compromises, some habits that each of us was willing to change.

The thing is, I so appreciate that tenderness of hers, how she watches out for me. When I become irritable and angry though, this deprives her of the joy of caring, and at the same time deprives me of allowing myself to feel cared about. And safe. Refusing her help serves only to diminish the pleasure we usually have when we're together. I'm working on that unlovely trait.

Besides allowing my vulnerability to be, to be seen, and being willing to receive coaching or help, some other strategies help counter those fears, get me back to center:

—Cultivating a positive attitude about it all is paramount. Lots of grateful thoughts about what I can still do, as well as acknowledging all the gifts in my life. A sense of humor goes a long way here. Lots of letting go too.

—Being of service in whatever ways possible.

—Being patient on those days when my physical challenges feel like they're about to take over my life. To diminish my life. I take it easy at those times, and compensate the best I can. And, given time, trust my usual resilience.

—Breathing deeply and often, pausing throughout the day. Not rushing about. I strive to live more mindfully—remembering to ask myself such questions as: do I need to change how I am viewing something or someone, or myself? I often examine my priorities: what really matters? In this moment … What really matters? Always, love is what rises to the top.

—Savoring solitude and quiet. Stillness. Time for reflection.

And at the same time … I love being with friends and family. And with the three children! The key is maintaining just the right balance of alone time and togetherness.

—Being ever alert for wayside poems. Every day, there is so much to marvel at—such sparkle at every turn. Simple things: looking out the window at my lively deck plants, walking along a nature path, marveling at the faces of loved ones as well as of strangers, playing with the children. It goes on and on. I seem in a constant state of wonder.

Each morning upon arising, I raise my arms high, gazing out at the open sky, and whisper, "Thank you for my life. Thank you for this day!" Then at sunset, I like to blow bubbles out on my deck.

And after the day is over, as I am falling asleep, I whisper a litany of thank yous for the gifts of the day. Especially do I cherish the presence of three precious children in my life, who in their nightly prayers say "God bless Rita."

I bless them too for sharing with me so many wondrous moments that have brought sweet music into my heart in this evening of my life. Their love has softened the edges around my whole world, as we have been walking six years through this book of life we've been writing together.

Some one of these days, I will pass the torch …

and leave, to another hand,

another voice,

the stories yet to be told …

For now, I am happy to be alive. To be old …

Next?

✧

Emma likes to keep careful track of everyone's age. We do this on my computer, listing in order: oldest person in the family to youngest, with age next to name. Every time a family member has a birthday, Emma reminds me to go to that family document. She's the one who gets to change the number to the accurate birthday age.

The children's Great Grandmother, 97 years old, known fondly as GG, is struggling with serious health issues. One afternoon Emma shares some sobering information with me: "Mommy says that GG might die pretty soon."

She pauses, her six-year-old mind tabulating ...

and follows with this question:

"And after GG dies, Rita, then ...

... then will you be next?"

My breath catches...

The question strikes a deep chord, there where my mortality, my advanced age, stare me full in the face. A profound, expansive, and sacred place it is, the purpose of my life on earth, with its reservoir of memories: all the milestones, stepping stones, times of brokenness unfolding into light...all the shoulders I've stood upon... my beloveds, here and gone... losses... the many glorious gifts, the countless blessings....

I stand in wonder and awe...

Deep breath...

"So ... **will** you be next, Rita?" Emma asks again, drawing me back from my reverie.

"Well I … I don't know, honey … Nobody knows …
Maybe … maybe I will be…
Maybe …"

Maybe not.

A "Good" Time

❦

Emma and I are falling asleep in her twin beds. A nightstand between us. Conscious of her breathing a few feet away, I match my breaths with hers. We lie there, saying nothing, breathing in the warm air, basking in the exquisite gift of stillness, of being together.

We've been in bed for about ten minutes, when Emma's soft voice breaks the silence: "Are you having a good time, Rita?"

I give what I soon realize is way too long an answer. "Oh yes, I've had a really good time with you today. We got to visit Curly the Camel and the two reindeer ... the Koi fish, and the train that had tracks along all the places in "Frozen." With Elsa and Ana standing at the doors of the castle ... When we came home, we had a terrific reading lesson, and after dinner you wrote three new stories! We've had a good time today."

"Yeah, but I mean are you having a good time since we got into bed?"

"Oh! Why yes, I am. We took our ten deep breaths together, didn't we, and I got to tuck you in. I told you the Golden Windows story. And now we are both toasty warm under the covers. You know, whenever I'm with you, here in your room, it is a good good time."

(Did I miss her point again?)

"Me too," she says. "I'm having a good time. I like you being over in my guest bed."

"Oh, I like that too," I tell her. "Okay, g'nite, honey. I love you."

"Love you too."

Emma and I do know what it means to share a " good" day as well as a "good" night. As I drift off to sleep, I'm reminded of Rabbi Abraham

Heschel's words, *"Just to be is a blessing. Just to live is holy."* *Just to be together is a blessing as well, and holy …*

❈

The next morning, before Emma leaves for Kindergarten, she wants to make sure I know something important, something about last night. She dresses quickly, digs out her crafts materials, and creates "a card" for me. Half of it is dark with stars and moon, for night. In the other half the sun is brightly shining: daytime.

The wise words of this little girl when she presents her card to me:

"Now on days when I'm in school or you don't see me, remember that I love you during the night and I love you during the day …

"And any time when you go away, put this card in your suitcase to remind you …"

I intend doing just that.

Epiphany

I leave the children's with yet another wad of love messages crumpled in my pocket. Even a rare one from Ethan in the form of a racetrack. Hugs all around and "I love yous" shouted as they close the door behind me. Emma at the window pointing to herself—then drawing a heart in the air—then pointing to me. Chloe grinning, hand to cheek. Ethan waving.

A daily ritual. And what I consistently write about. "Didn't you say this in one of your stories several pages ago?" I did. Same ole same ole you are suggesting? Never. Ever. Always I treasure these moments. They give me goose bumps.

Today, as I am driving away, something shifts …

I find myself in a strange inner space,

>   far beyond the seat in my car.

In a flash I begin seeing the world in a whole new way,

>   through a greatly magnified lens,

>   as if I am *inside* everything I behold …

>   and at the same time—

>   as if from a place above, peering down …

My senses become more acute than ever before …

>   every color more vivid …

>   every sound amplified

feeling so profound I can scarcely breathe.

>   and then … I can …

>   slow and easy.

Everything my glance falls upon seems intensified:

    forsythia shouting yellow to the sky …

        clusters of daffodils …

I look into their faces …

        feel a part of each one

    as though seeing them for the first time …

    Or could it be my last?

        All of a sudden I realized I was driving.

        "Rita! You will miss all of this if you keep going.

        You need to stop the car, and be present.

        Pay attention."

I simply pulled over and sat quietly. Did nothing.

My mind seemed empty—silent and receptive.

Just take it in, Rita. Become one with it …

Moments—perhaps hours—passed.

  Timeless. Eternal…

        like a reprieve …

            like I'd been told I was dying soon,

                and almost had …

  Then discovered I was alive.

    So alive.

"The gentlest sense of wholeness and down-deep satisfaction came over me, greater than I have ever known. It enfolded me like a warm mist and calmed me to the core … a feeling of being totally, quietly, completely alive. Then I realized what it was: I was happy. Happy. That's all. Just happy …

"It felt within me like the stillness of an inland lake. I looked back over all the open meadows and tangled underbrush of my life and knew in an instant, like the snap of a shutter on a digital camera, that whatever had been, it had been right. Where I had been born was right, how I had lived life had been right, even all its wrong parts had been right."

~from *Following the Path, the Search for a Life of Passion, Purpose and Joy*

by Joan Chittister

Legacy: "I can write a story!"

❧

"Mommy just gave me this book," Emma tells me. "It's empty. What do you think I should do with it?"

"Well, you could start writing stories in it."

"I can write a story?"

"You sure can."

So we begin.

On the first page, she writes the date.

"Shall I put whether it is day or night?"

"You are the writer, and the writer gets to do whatever she wants."

"Whatever I want?"

"Umhmmm."

"Okay, I want to put that it is night time when I start this."

Thus begins her first story:

"November 10, 2014

at night 8:30

I LOVE YOU ..."

And we go on from there.

We write a little story each week

maybe only two or three short sentences, like:

My Car

"My car is a mini-van.

It can fit 7 people!

The van is gray.

I like listening to the music

and I like singing along with it."

Emma always decorates each story, this one with a van

rolling along the street, music notes streaming out from it.

❀

I've often wondered what legacy

I might leave.

Oh I know, the books I have written will live on …

and grad students I've chanced to meet

some 25 years later

remind me of classes I taught

and wisdoms they carry with them

still today

in their professions … and in their lives.

Yet, I've wondered …

    … until …

one day, after Emma spotted two tiny eggs

    in a bird's nest

on one of the low branches of a tall cedar,

    she comes running to me, breathless:

"Rita Rita! Can I write a story about that?"

    Now *that* is a legacy I cherish.

Upward

Sweet voices of light pulse through me
in a continuous streaming…
from the depths where all that is,
resides.

The song that is mine alone to sing
crescendos,
my spirit flourishes,
even as I feel the fullness
of some 82 years
creeping through my bones.

They say that as you age…
you peak…peak…
and then…

o

v

e

r

the hill you go…
down…

d

  o

    w

      n…

That may be true for this flesh
  in the garden of dust…

    not so—
   for my spirit…

Upward it soars,
  breathless
ever spiraling
  in cosmic circles
across the sky…

on clouds of remembering:
  the vast stillness and glory
    from which we come
      and to which we return…
        beginning and ending
        intertwined

in this moment …

this day …

this life …

Soaring spiraling dancing singing

into The Great Light

into the Light … the Light …

into the sweet Light …

A Blessing

for Children,

    for Parents,

        for You the Reader

            for Every Person on This Planet

May you be at peace

May your heart remain open

May you awaken to the light of your own true nature

May you be healed

May you be a source of healing for the world.

~Tibetan Buddhist Prayer

Resources

As a psychologist with specialized training in working with children and their parents, I am suggesting some resources that may be helpful along the way. This is only a fragment of what is available, and is in no way considered comprehensive.

Many resources are right at your fingertips, i.e. in your public library. For instance, the **Seattle Public Library** (*www.slp.org*) offers two-page booklists/print-outs "For children and families" in which they list books that are available on "Sensitive Issues" such as Self-Confidence, Divorce, Moving, Bullying, Adoption, Death.
Both fiction and non-fiction are listed.

THERE ARE A NUMBER OF OTHER TOPICS IMPORTANT TO MENTION:

"Making Caring Common Project."
Harvard University (Graduate School of Education) study "aims to strengthen the abilities of parents and caretakers, schools and community members to develop caring, ethical children. We are working to make these values live and breathe in the day-to-day interactions of every school and home."
Sign up for their newsletter "Strategies and Tips for Parents and Caretakers" *www.gse.harvard.edu/making-caring-common*

Mindful Self-Compassion (MSC). Affiliated with Harvard Medical School, Dr. Kristin Neff: Compares Self-compassion with self-esteem.

Love & Logic Strategies: Keys for Better Parenting website

MINDFULNESS:
I wish I had learned about the practice of mindfulness when I was in training to be a teacher, and later a counselor. I am happy to report that now many university psychology programs, including the University of Washington, include it in their syllabus.

Mindfulness resources:

Second Step: a socio-emotional program which utilizes many of the practices of mindfulness such as

—remembering to Breathe.

—Learning how to change my attitude, shift my perception, manage my emotions and my thoughts.

"The Slow Tech Movement"

Related to mindfulness, and gaining momentum..." **Slow Tech** parenting is about awareness. It's about knowing what works for your family, what aligns with your values...

Find excellent ideas in an article by Janell Burley Hoffman, syndicated from huffingtonpost.com April 17, 2015. Suggests boundaries, or iRules—specific ways we can use the technology without it taking over our lives.

Spiritual Parenting in the Digital Age

www.spiritualityandpractice.com/.../spiritual-parenting-in-the-digital-age

Bullying/Unkind Behavior:

It seems like a day doesn't go by without news of some sort of bullying incident. That's really no surprise when you consider that over *70 percent of students say they have witnessed bullying happening in their schools.*

I was stunned to learn that bullying in preschool has escalated in the past five years...

Some excellent articles can be found on line, e.g.

The Ophelia Project: "A Relational Aggression Curriculum: sticking up for yourself."

Eight Keys to End Bullying by Signe Whitson, syndicated from *Greated Good*, Oct 25, 2014

How Not to Deal with Bullying (from Care2common causes)

The Family Virtues Guide: *Simple Ways to Bring Out the Best in Our Children and Ourselves* by Linda Kavelin Popov. This book does not deal with such topics as "anti-bullying," but rather stresses "promoting kindness" and other practices.

CREATIVITY:

If a rare open day in the summer happens along, the children when asked, "Where shall we go?" inevitably choose: "Stay at home." Only thing is then, it drives Mommy or the nanny crazy. They do need to get out.
However, if they stay at home, engaging in crafts is a marvelous option for most.

A recent UCLA study found that when young people engage in the arts at an early age, they outperform their peers in every category, from academics to life skills.
Numerous studies show that activities like drawing and creative writing also raise serotonin levels and decrease anxiety.
Adapted from *Catch the Fire: An Art-Full Guide to Unleashing the Creative Power of Youth, Adults and Communities* by Peggy Taylor and Charlie Murphy for **Education Uprising**, the Spring 2014 issue of *YES!* Magazine. Published by New Society Publishers, January 2014.

Beautiful Oops: inspires art projects; and learning from mistakes.

About the Author

Rita Bresnahan has always loved children. Growing up, she delighted in playing junior mom to three sibs who were nine, eleven, and thirteen years younger than she.

Rita has devoted nearly all of her professional life to making a difference in the lives of children. With a B.A. in Education, for sixteen years she taught children in elementary and secondary grades throughout central Illinois.

She earned a Master's in Social Work from the University of Illinois, specializing in children's issues. For five years she served as Associate Director of the Children's Division in the Boulder Mental Health Center, where she conducted child therapy sessions and parenting classes. During the same years she served as mental health liaison to elementary schools and to the Early Childhood Centers of Boulder County, as well as working with special education issues.

A Seattle psychologist, social worker, and educator, her real-life stories reflect the meaning, and often the poetry, she finds in everyday kinds of happenings—through her favored themes of insight and transformation, children, and humor.

Rita is author of *Walking One Another Home: Moments of Grace and Possibility in the Midst of Alzheimer's* and of *Listening to the Corn: the heartbeats of life all around.*

Her work has appeared in such works as *Chicken Soup for the Woman's Soul* and in *A Time to Weep, A Time to Sing: Faith Journeys of Women Scholars of Religion.*

Rita can be reached at *namaste7@comcast.net*

For more about the author, see the Ballard Writers Collective website:

www.ballardwriters.org/2013/01/13/rita